The Best of Teresa Wentzler
Sampler Collection

Welcome to the fascinating world of Teresa Wentzler! This leaflet showcases nine of Teresa's wonderfully intricate cross stitch samplers for seasonal décor and special occasions. And we've even included two fantasy and fable samplers, just for fun! Take a walk through a glorious English garden or play your flute to enchant a dragon. Then sample the joyful abundance of autumn and the thrill of a magical Christmas. You'll transcend reality through the vivid details of every piece! After more than a decade of producing outstanding cross stitch designs, Teresa continues to make her art fresh with discovery, inspiring stitching enthusiasts all over the world. Fabulous borders and a bounty of specialty stitches, beads, floss, and metallic threads enrich Teresa's imaginative themes. Her unique design style combines the play of light with subtle shadings of color, accomplishing a visual depth that keeps stitchers coming back for more. Revel in the luxury of creating your own Teresa Wentzler masterpieces. You'll love every stitch!

LEISURE ARTS, INC.
Little Rock, Arkansas

Teresa Wentzler

From time to time, Teresa gives way to daydreams that eventually become the inspiration for new designs. "When new ideas pop into my head, many times I'm able to apply them immediately. There are always several designs in progress at one time."

There's always a story behind the elements in Teresa Wentzler's intricate designs. When asked to recall her inspiration for the designs in this collection, Teresa chuckles.

"One idea came from a photo I saw in a local newspaper. They were having old-fashioned sleigh races, and one sleigh was so perfectly nostalgic, it found its way into the *Christmas Sampler*."

And while gathering research for the *English Cottage Sampler*, she was fascinated to learn that "English thatchers each have a different way of cutting the straw on a roof. The pattern they use to finish a roof identifies their work, and a thatched roof can last a hundred years." Teresa portrayed this craftsmanship carefully on the house in her sampler.

"I love looking at the old homes in England," she says, "and I look forward to a trip there soon."

The jousting knights in the *Camelot Sampler* are an example of the attention to detail that has made Teresa famous in needlecraft circles — each cross stitch is worked over just one thread. And she often includes a number of specialty stitches to further enrich

...e texture of her compositions, as ...the delicate *Heart Sampler*.

Of her work, Teresa says, "My ...vorite subjects are things I can pull ...om my imagination or anything ...ith which I may take creative ...ense. I love to do the unexpected ...ith a design. If it can make a ...itcher feel as if he ...she is taking part ...an 'alternate ...ality,' even if only ...r a moment, then I ...onsider it 'good,' ...d I'm satisfied."

An avid reader of ...ntasy novels since ...e was in high ...hool, Teresa gets ...esign ideas from ...lected classics, ...ry tales, fables, ...d stories of the ...aranormal. As an ...tist, she also draws ...eative inspiration ...om the pre-Raphael ...tists, from children's ...ok illustrators ...the late 1800's ...d early 1900's, ...d from arts and ...afts trends.

Considering such ...fluences from ...erature and art ...story, it's not ...rprising that the two combine in ...r designs. "I've done artwork ...er since I can remember," she ...ys. "When I was a child, I used to ...aw these really strange, abstract ...nds of drawings."

After graduating from high ...hool, Teresa knew that she "wanted ...do something with art, but didn't ...ow what." She went to college ...d studied fine arts for a year, but ...ithdrew and married Carl, now ...r husband of 19 years. She returned ...community college four years later and earned an associate's degree in advertising art. This training, she says, "definitely helped prepare me for the 'art' end of designing — the realities of deadlines, 'art-on-demand,' and other aspects of production such as charting and writing instructions."

> "My favorite subjects are things I can pull from my imagination or anything with which I may take creative license. I love to do the unexpected with a design. If it can make a stitcher feel as if he or she is taking part in an 'alternate reality,' even if only for a moment, then I consider it 'good,' and I'm satisfied."

Teresa happened upon success unexpectedly in 1985. "I couldn't find the type of designs that I wanted to stitch as gifts for friends, so I did them myself. I didn't do it with a career in mind. I didn't even realize one could design for a living."

Today, Teresa's cross stitch charts have appeared in more than 60 leaflets, numerous kits, and in several books and magazines.

"Realistic fantasy" is the term Teresa uses to describe her style, adding, "I like to render imaginary subjects with as much realism as possible. If the subject is not an imaginary one, I try very hard to add something that will give it some extra 'zing,' such as a decorative border."

A piece of ribbon on the brim of a hat inspired part of the border design she created for the *Harvest Sampler*. "With a change in color," she says, "the motif on the ribbon was reborn into the serpentine pattern at top and bottom."

Teresa says her designing process is a tedious one because she doesn't actually do artwork or finished art. "I usually just do a black and white sketch, with a bit of a value study, which I submit for approval. I then transfer the idea directly to graph paper where I'm able to work out all the details of composition and color."

The Internet and e-mail have allowed the artist to receive a lot of input and ideas from fans. "Most of my designs are now taken directly from the stitchers' requests that are posted on the bulletin board at my Web site," she says. Her Web address is **www.twdesignworks.com**, and her e-mail address is **tlw@microserve.net**.

Surfing the Internet is something Teresa likes to do, especially since it enables her to "keep up with what's new in the needlework industry." She also enjoys stitching,

From her home studio that's "chock-full of designing paraphernalia," Teresa reveals she believes that serious stitchers love a challenge. "It's very fortunate for me because I really like 'the edge' and love to 'push the envelope' in cross stitch design."

knitting, listening to music, reading, walking, drawing, and painting — all from her Pennsylvania home. Having lived in the state her whole life, Teresa points out that she, her husband, and their cats, Tom and Jake, appreciate "all the charm of rural life, with the conveniences of town not far away."

Since she works from a small studio in her home that's "chock-full of designing paraphernalia," Teresa reveals that she gets to be creative all the time. "When new ideas pop into my head, many times I'm able to apply them immediately. There are always several designs in progress at one time."

There's another kind of art that's of interest to Teresa. "I truly appreciate 'pure art,' or doing art for its own sake, but I have very little free time to devote to it. I hope to someday be able to sit down and draw and paint for the sheer joy of doing so."

Nevertheless, Teresa is quick to acknowledge the pleasure she finds in what she's chosen to do for now. "I'm very lucky in that what I love to design, quite a few people like to stitch, either for themselves or as gifts. I also believe that, for the most part, serious stitchers love a challenge, which is very fortunate for me because I really like 'the edge' and love to 'push the envelope' in cross stitch design."

Reflecting on her accomplishments of the last 15 years, Teresa's voice softens. "When I'm working on a difficult design and I come across one of my earlier charts, one that I've almost forgotten, it surprises me. I look at it and think 'Oh, I did that!' and then I know I can do this — I can finish my new design." Hearing her modest pride, it's impossible not to rejoice right along with her.

TABLE OF CONTENTS

	Photo	Chart
Harvest Sampler	6	24
Camelot Sampler	8	30
Fantasy Sampler	10	45
English Cottage Sampler	12	50
English Garden Sampler	14	60
Birth Announcement	16	71
Christmas Sampler	18	78
Wedding Sampler	20	84
Heart Sampler	22	90
General Instructions		94

Copyright© 2001 by Leisure Arts, Inc., 5701 Ranch Drive, Little Rock, Arkansas 72223-9633. All rights reserved. Visit our Web site at www.leisurearts.com. No part of this book may be reproduced in any form or by any means without the prior written permission of the publisher, except for brief quotations in reviews appearing in magazines or newspapers. We have made every effort to ensure that these instructions are accurate and complete. We cannot, however, be responsible for human error, typographical mistakes, or variations in individual work. Made in the United States of America.

EDITORIAL STAFF — *Vice President and Editor-at-Large:* Anne Van Wagner Childs. *Vice President and Editor-in-Chief:* Sandra Case. *Director of Designer Relations:* Debra Nettles. *Editorial Director:* Susan Frantz Wiles. *Publications Director:* Susan White Sullivan. *Creative Art Director:* Gloria Bearden. *Art Operations Director:* Jeff Curtis. **PRODUCTION** — *Managing Editor:* Mary Sullivan Hutcheson. *Senior Editor:* Karen Jackson. *Assistant Editors:* Carolyn Breeding, Mimi Harrington, Joyce Scott Holland, and Laura Siar Holyfield. **EDITORIAL** — *Managing Editor:* Suzie Puckett. *Associate Editor:* Susan McManus Johnson. **ART** — *Senior Art Director:* Rhonda Hodge Shelby. *Color Technician:* Mark Hawkins. *Senior Production Artist:* Lora Puls. *Production Artists:* Shalana Fleetwood, Deborah Kelly, and John Rose. *Publishing Systems Administrator:* Becky Riddle. *Publishing Systems Assistants:* Myra S. Means and Chris Wertenberger.

BUSINESS STAFF — *Publisher:* Rick Barton. *Vice President, Finance:* Tom Siebenmorgen. *Director of Corporate Planning and Development:* Laticia Mull Cornett. *Vice President, Retail Marketing:* Bob Humphrey. *Vice President, Sales:* Ray Shelgosh. *Vice President, National Accounts:* Pam Stebbins. *Director of Sales and Service:* Margaret Sweetin. *Vice President, Operations:* Jim Dittrich. *Comptroller, Operations:* Rob Thieme. *Retail Customer Service Manager:* Wanda Price. *Print Production Manager:* Fred F. Pruss.

Softcover ISBN 1-57486-236-7

10 9 8 7 6 5 4 3 2 1

For more of Teresa's wonderful designs, including *The Castle* and *The Castle Sampler*, see *The Best of Teresa Wentzler — Fantasy Collection* (Leisure Arts Item #15872, ISBN 1-57486-186-7).

Harvest Sampler

Waving in the breeze, ripened grains of wheat await the harvest. Tart apples will soon become a freshly baked pie, and fading boughs of laurel crown autumn as queen of the seasons. Over it all, an abundance of specialty stitches and glass seed beads enrich the dignified sampler. Never before have the scenes and shades of fall been so serenely rendered.

Chart begins on page 24.

CAMELOT SAMPLER

BRING ENGLAND'S BEST-LOVED TALE OF CHIVALRY AND ROMANCE TO LIFE ON A CHEVRON-SHAPED SAMPLER. GOOD KING ARTHUR AND THE BEAUTIFUL GUINEVERE LOOK OUT OVER THEIR REALM WITH HOPE FOR A GLORIOUS FUTURE. BETWEEN THEM STANDS EXCALIBUR, THE SWORD ONLY THE ONE TRUE KING COULD WIELD. WORKED OVER ONE THREAD FOR EXQUISITE DETAIL, JOUSTING KNIGHTS DISPLAY THE WARRIOR SKILLS THAT DEFENDED CAMELOT FOR A BRIEF BUT SHINING TIME. METALLIC BLENDING FILAMENTS ADD RICHNESS TO THIS ENCHANTING TAPESTRY.

Chart begins on page 30.

Fantasy Sampler

As a brave maiden pipes a mesmerizing tune, an enchanted dragon pauses — he's never heard such wondrous sounds — and lies down at the musician's feet. Now you can use needle and floss to capture your own magical beasts from myth and legend! See a winged Pegasus leap into the air while a noble unicorn enjoys his freedom. A golden griffin stands as a fearsome sentry. And like the maiden's dragon, Androcles' lion is ready to be tamed by a courageous heart.

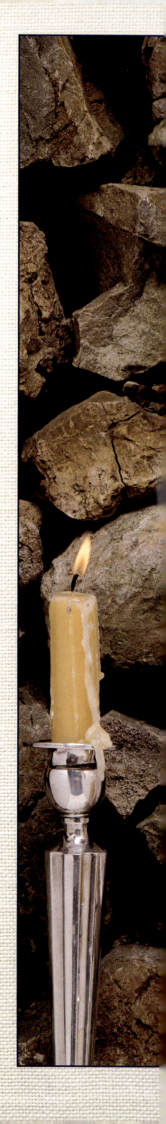

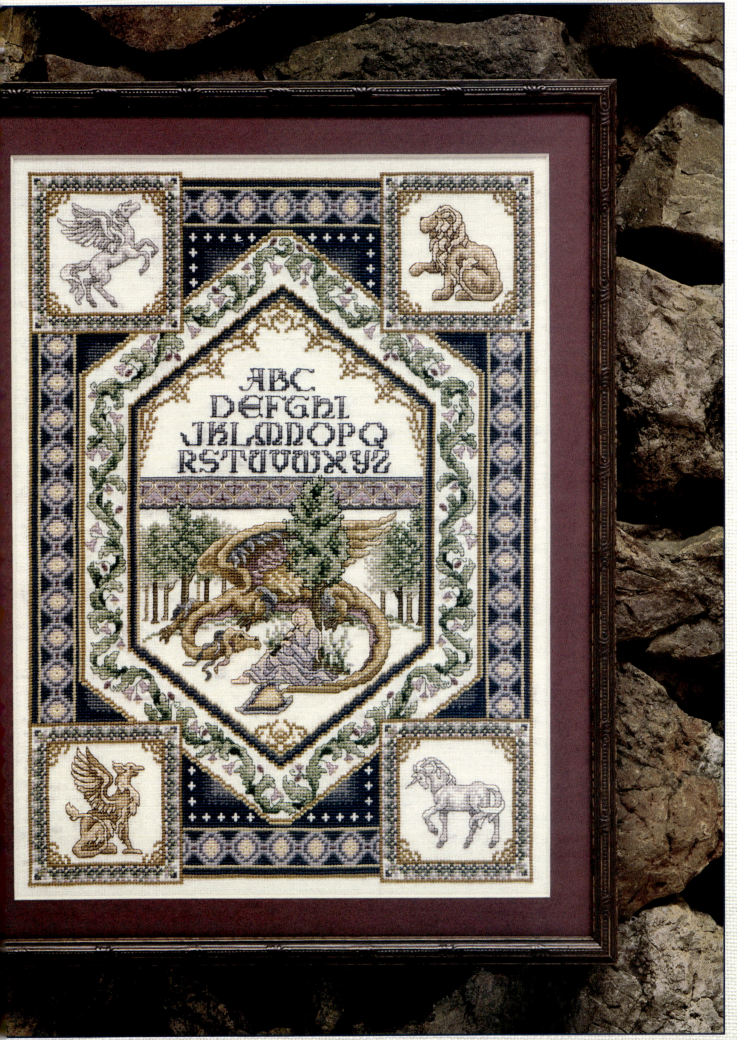

ENGLISH COTTAGE SAMPLER

PAMPER YOURSELF WITH THE TRANQUIL VIEW OF A CHARMING COTTAGE NESTLED IN THE QUIET ENGLISH COUNTRYSIDE. NOT TOO LARGE AND NOT TOO SMALL, THIS THATCHED ABODE IS JUST RIGHT FOR HOUSING YOUR DAYDREAMS. FLOWERING VINES GLISTEN WITH GLASS BEADS AS THEY TWINE ALL ABOUT THE SAMPLER, ENCLOSING A VIGNETTE OF GRACEFUL SWANS AND TWO ARTFUL ALPHABETS. YOU'LL CHERISH THE MEMORIES OF "BUILDING" YOUR VERY OWN ENGLISH COTTAGE SAMPLER FOR MANY YEARS TO COME.

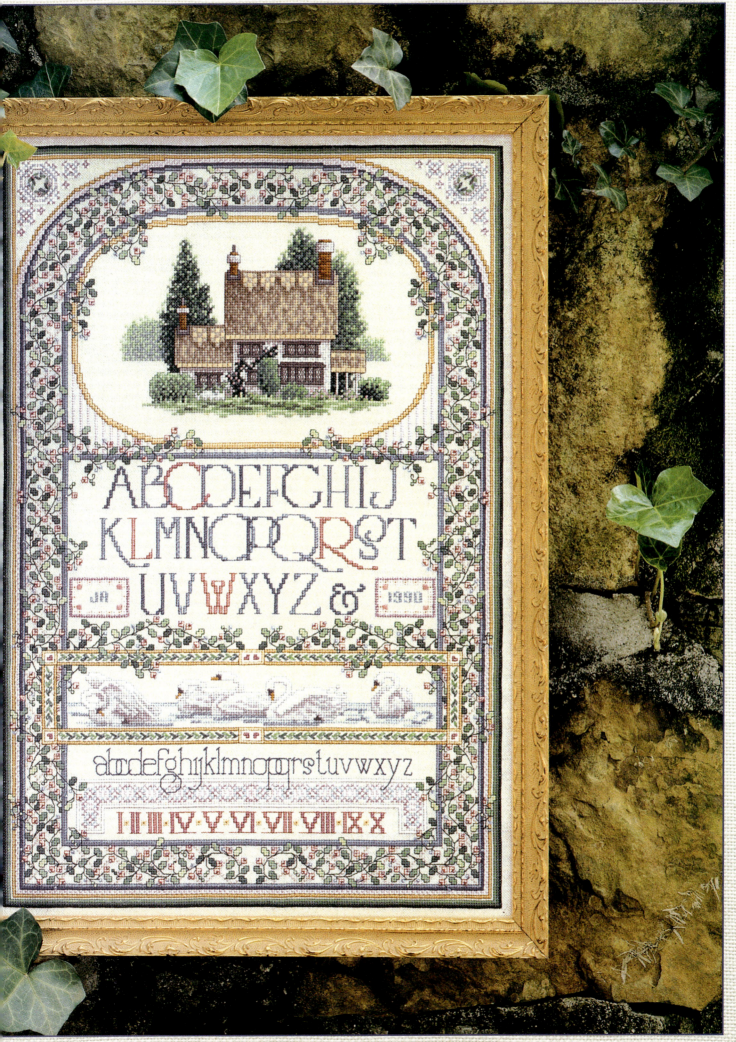

Chart begins on page 50.

ENGLISH GARDEN SAMPLER

STEP INSIDE THE FILIGREE GATE TO DISCOVER A FLAWLESS GARDEN OF MANICURED SHRUBS AND SCULPTURED TOPIARIES — ALL THRIVING UNDER A MISTY ENGLISH SKY. SHIMMERING PEACOCKS GREET STROLLING VISITORS WITH THEIR EXOTIC SONG. THE CALMING SOUND OF FALLING WATER LEADS TO A MARBLE FOUNTAIN BANKED BY A BOXWOOD HEDGE. ALL AROUND, DRIFTS OF BLOOMING WISTERIA AND ROWS OF LAVENDER FILL THE AIR WITH THE SWEET, HEADY FRAGRANCE OF EARLY SUMMER. THIS SPLENDID SAMPLER IS SELF-MATTED WITH A DOUBLE BORDER OF HEMSTITCHES AND TINY EYELETS. METALLIC CORD, GLASS SEED BEADS, AND PEARL COTTON INDULGE THE STITCHER'S DESIRE FOR LIFE'S FINER THINGS.

Chart begins on page 60.

Birth Announcement

FROM THEIR PEACEFUL GARDEN REPOSE, ANGELS GLANCE SKYWARD AND REJOICE. NEWS OF A MOMENTOUS EVENT IS PROUDLY INSCRIBED ACROSS THE BLUE VAULT OF HEAVEN. AN IDEAL GIFT FOR A NEW MOTHER, THIS MASTERPIECE OF INTRICATE STITCHES, DELICATE SHADINGS, AND SHINING BEADWORK CELEBRATES THE JOYOUS ARRIVAL OF ONE OF GOD'S MOST PRECIOUS CREATIONS — A BABY!

Chart begins on page 71.

Christmas Sampler

You can almost hear the merry jingle bells as this regal sleigh passes by. Eyelet-stitch snowflakes flutter down upon the benevolent princess as she prepares to leave the castle pavilions. Holly and mistletoe, sprinkled with tiny bead "berries," form a traditional yuletide border, while festive bows hold an elegant garland. With a word to her sure-footed companion, her majesty is off to make a very special delivery of holiday joy.

Chart begins on page 78.

Wedding Sampler

Unite the names of the blissful newlyweds on a romantic sampler! Beneath an arched colonnade and amid sumptuous blossoms, tiny stitches form the wedding proclamation. Ribbon-wrapped festoons of greenery soften the formal border, while glass beads shine forever on this stunning commemoration of a truly wonderful occasion.

Chart begins on page 84.

HEART SAMPLER

HERE'S A CHARMING SAMPLER TO WARM THE HEART OF ANY ACCOMPLISHED STITCHER. THE LIGHT-AND-LACY LOOK IS CREATED BY A BOUNTY OF STITCHES AND TECHNIQUES, INCLUDING HARDANGER AND CUTWORK. GLASS SEED BEADS ARE ADDED FOR A SPARKLING FINISH. THE LOVELY PIECE IS EASILY ALTERED TO MAKE A BEAUTIFUL BRIDAL GIFT, AS WELL. SIMPLY INCLUDE THE INITIALS OF THE HAPPY COUPLE AND ADD THE WEDDING DATE ON THE OTHER SIDE OF THE HEART.

Chart begins on page 90.

Harvest Sampler

Our model was stitched over two fabric threads on 28 count Bone Brittney fabric from Zweigart®, using 2 strands of floss for Cross Stitches and Specialty Stitches, 1 strand of each color floss for Blended Cross Stitches, Blended Specialty Stitches, Blended Backstitches, and 1 strand for Backstitches and Specialty Stitches using Pearl Cotton unless noted. Alphabets and numbers are provided for personalization. *We recommend stitching the design in the order listed.*

Stitch Count: 144w x 193h
Design Size:
25 ct fabric (over 2 threads) $11\frac{5}{8}$" x $15\frac{1}{2}$"
28 ct fabric (over 2 threads) $10\frac{3}{8}$" x $13\frac{7}{8}$"
32 ct fabric (over 2 threads) 9"   x $12\frac{1}{8}$"

Cross Stitch

Symbol	DMC	COLOR
••	ecru	ecru
−	ecru / blanc	ecru / white
+	ecru / 739	ecru / vy lt tan
<	353 / 950	peach flesh / lt coco brown
D	370 / 3363	dk pecan / loden green
L	371 / 3052	pecan / med grey green
∕	372 / 3013	lt pecan / lt kahki green
∩	422	lt hazelnut brown
I	422 / 739	lt hazelnut brown / vy lt tan
⊙	422 / 3045	lt hazelnut brown / dk yellow beige
	640	vy dk beige grey
Z	842	vy lt beige brown
✄	3032	med mocha brown
P	3041	med antique violet
V	3041 / 3042	med antique violet / lt antique violet
X	3045	dk yellow beige
◐	3045 / 3782	dk yellow beige / lt mocha brown
	3740	dk antique violet
S	3773 / 3778	med sportsman flesh / lt terra cotta
⊗	30738	old gold rayon

DMC Pearl Cotton
ecru #12

DMC Rayon Floss
30738   old gold

MILL HILL GLASS SEED BEADS
● 0557 gold
¢ 3005 platinum rose

Attach gold beads using 1 strand DMC 422.
Attach platinum rose beads using 1 strand DMC 3773.
Add beads after all other stitching is complete.

Outer Border
1. Work Cross Stitch
Note: Blocks around small flowers are for placement only and are not to be Backstitched.
2. ∕ 30738   net pattern
3. ✺ ecru / 739   Large Diamond Eyelet Stitch
4. ᴑ 370 / 3363   Lazy Daisy Stitch
5. ᴑ 371 / 3052   Lazy Daisy Stitch
6. ∕ 640   outside edge

Serpentine Rows
Note: Blocks around small flowers are for placement only and are not to be Backstitched.
1. Work Cross Stitch
2. ∕ 640   medallions
3. ∕ 422 / 3045   serpentine motif
4. Wrap 422/3045 Backstitch using 30738 (**1** strand).
5. ∕ 371 / 3052   stems
6. ᴑ 371 / 3052   Lazy Daisy Stitch
7. ∕ 30738   net pattern
8. ✺ ecru / 739   Medium Diamond Eyelet Stitch
9. ✳ ecru / 739   Large Smyrna Cross Stitch
10. ✳ 422 / 739   Large Smyrna Cross Stitch

1. ✱ 3045 (**2** strands) Algerian Eye Stitch
2. ✱ [422 / 739] Diamond Smyrna Stitch
3. ✱ 3045 (**2** strands) Large Smyrna Cross Stitch
4. ✱ [422 / 739] Very Small Diamond Eyelet Stitch

Wheat Row
Work Cross Stitch
- / [422 / 3045] wheat (long stitches)
- / 640 wheat
- / 3045 wheat

Alphabet Row
Work Cross Stitch
- / 640 D, H, N, P, T, and Y
- / 3041 A, C, E, G, I, K, M, O, Q, S, U, W, and Z
- / 3740 B, F, J, L, R, V, and X

Small Leaf Row
- ▨ [370 / 3363] Scotch Stitch
- ▨ [371 / 3052] Scotch Stitch
- / 370 stems

Apple Row
Work Cross Stitch
- / 370 leaves
- / 640 apples (**1** strand) and stems (**2** strands)

Numeral Row
1. Work Cross Stitch
2. / 3740

Date and Initial Blocks
1. [422 / 3045] Plaited Cross Stitch in corner blocks
2. ⦀ [422 / 739] Satin Stitch
3. / [371 / 3052] initials and year

Row A
ecru #12 Pearl Cotton Herringbone Stitch

Row B
ecru #12 Pearl Cotton Three-Sided Stitch

Row C
ecru #12 Pearl Cotton Barrier Stitch

Row D
ecru #12 Pearl Cotton Long-Armed Cross Stitch

Row E
ecru #12 Pearl Cotton work 39 Horizontal Knitting Stitches beginning at left. Continue row with 39 Horizontal Knitting Stitches in reverse to complete second half of row.

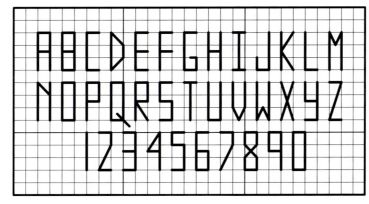

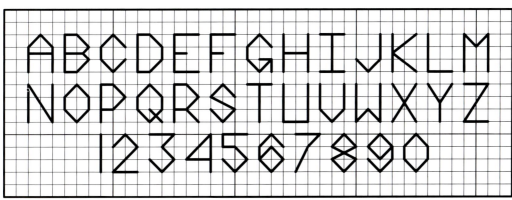

ALPHABETS AND NUMBERS

HARVEST SAMPLER SECTION 1

haded rows indicate overlap from Section 1.

ARVEST SAMPLER SECTION 2

Shaded rows indicate overlap from Section 1.

HARVEST SAMPLER SECTION 3

HARVEST SAMPLER SECTION 4

Camelot Sampler

Our model was stitched over two fabric threads on 25 count Bone Lugana fabric from Zweigart®, using 2 strands of floss for Cross Stitches, 1 strand of each color floss for Blended Cross Stitches, Blended Backstitches, and Blended Lazy Daisy Stitches, and 1 strand for Backstitches and all Specialty Stitches unless noted. Use 1 strand of floss for Cross Stitches and Backstitches over one fabric thread unless noted. Alphabets and numbers are provided for personalization. *Because of the Cross Stitches and Backstitches worked over one fabric thread, this design is not suitable for stitching on Aida fabric.*

Stitch Count: 138w x 208h
Design Size: 25 ct fabric (over 2 threads) 11⅛" x 16¾"
28 ct fabric (over 2 threads) 9⅞" x 14⅞"
32 ct fabric (over 2 threads) 8⅝" x 13"

Cross Stitch

Symbol	DMC	COLOR
!	blanc	white
⋋	ecru	ecru
⌐	224	lt shell pink
∧	225	vy lt shell pink
&	304	Christmas red
@	315	dk antique mauve
R	[315 / 3041	dk antique mauve / antique violet
E	316	antique mauve
≠	[316 / 3042	antique mauve / lt antique violet
○	317	pewter grey
✗	318	lt steel grey
⌐	[318 / 414	lt steel grey / dk steel grey
⌐	[318 / 3042	lt steel grey / lt antique violet
n	[318 / 3743	lt steel grey / vy lt antique violet
	319	vy dk pistachio green
⌐	413	dk pewter grey
⌐	414	dk steel grey
H	[414 / 3042	dk steel grey / lt antique violet
ω	415	pearl grey
≈	[415 / 3743	pearl grey / vy lt antique violet
★	420	dk hazelnut brown
X	422	lt hazelnut brown
⊕	[422 / 676	lt hazelnut brown / lt old gold
£	[422 / 3828	lt hazelnut brown / hazelnut brown
4	433	brown
⊙	434	lt brown
○	435	vy lt brown
⌐	436	tan
N	451	dk shell grey
⊢	[451 / 452	dk shell grey / shell grey
X	452	shell grey
⌐	[452 / 453	shell grey / lt shell grey
?	453	lt shell grey
ℓ	[453 / 762	lt shell grey / vy lt pearl grey

Cross Stitch

Symbol	DMC	COLOR
⊥	500	vy dk blue green
⌐	[500 / 520	vy dk blue green / dk olive drab
%	501	dk blue green
⌐	[501 / 3362	dk blue green / dk loden green
⌐	502	blue green
○	[502 / 522	blue green / olive drab
n	[502 / 3363	blue green / loden green
∈	503	blue green
♡	[503 / 523	blue green / med olive drab
e	504	lt blue green
∙∙	[504 / 524	lt blue green / lt olive drab
⊔	520	dk olive drab
□	522	olive drab
⌐	[522 / 3052	olive drab / med grey green
÷	523	med olive drab
¶	[523 / 3053	med olive drab / grey green
⊞	610	vy dk drab brown
W	611	dk drab brown
△	612	med drab brown
d	613	lt drab brown
	640	vy dk beige grey
3	676	lt old gold
=	677	vy lt old gold
♥	680	dk old gold
♦	729	med old gold
<	738	vy lt tan
L	739	ul vy lt tan
a	758	lt terra cotta
μ	760	salmon
:	762	vy lt pearl grey
⌐	[762 / 3743	vy lt pearl grey / vy lt antique violet
¢	778	lt antique mauve
Κ	791	vy dk cornflower blue
φ	[791 / 3750	vy dk cornflower blue / vy dk antique blue
+	792	dk cornflower blue

Cross Stitch

Symbol	DMC	COLOR
z	[792 / 930	dk cornflower blue / dk antique blue
¥	793	med cornflower blue
∂	[793 / 931	med cornflower blue / med antique blue
«	794	lt cornflower blue
r	[794 / 932	lt cornflower blue / lt antique blue
▲	801	dk coffee brown
✧	814	dk garnet
@	815	med garnet
Æ	816	garnet
2	818	baby pink
−	819	lt baby pink
⊖	840	med beige brown
ℵ	841	lt beige brown
·|·	842	vy lt beige brown
✗	898	vy dk coffee brown
9	930	dk antique blue
◁	931	med antique blue
A	932	lt antique blue
⊥	950	lt coco brown
≡	3011	dk khaki green
∀	3012	med khaki green
±	3013	lt khaki green
#	3032	med mocha brown
⊃	3033	vy lt mocha brown
⊟	3041	med antique violet
⊖	[3041 / 3726	med antique violet / dk antique mauve
▼	[3041 / 3740	med antique violet / dk antique violet
◇	3042	lt antique violet
∪	[3042 / 3727	lt antique violet / lt antique mauve
⌐	[3042 / 3743	lt antique violet / vy lt antique violet
8	3045	dk yellow beige
K	[3051 / 3052	dk grey green / med grey green
⌐	3052	med grey green
φ	3053	grey green
M	3064	spice
●	3362	dk loden green
⌐	[3362 / 3363	dk loden green / loden green

30

Cross Stitch

DMC	COLOR
3363	loden green
3713	vy lt salmon
3726	dk antique mauve
3727	lt antique mauve
3740	dk antique violet
⎡3740	dk antique violet
⎣3802	deep antique mauve
3743	vy lt antique violet
⎡3747	vy lt blue violet
⎣3752	vy lt antique violet
3770	vy lt flesh
3773	med sportsman flesh
3774	vy lt sportsman flesh
3782	lt mocha brown
3807	cornflower blue
3823	ul pale yellow
3828	hazel nut brown
712	cream #12 pearl cotton

Half Cross Stitch

DMC	COLOR
415	pearl grey
3032	med mocha brown
3782	lt mocha brown

Backstitch

outer border
- 611   corner motifs, border, twisted rope
- ⎡422   border from bottom of jousting scene
- ⎣3828   to point above bottom motif

Note: Wrap 422/3828 Backstitch using 611 (**1** strand).
- 3032   border, twisted rope

jousting scene
- 611   borders
- 318   helmets (**2** strands), background scene

Arthur
- 611   crown, borders, clothing
- 640   face detail
- 792   lettering
- 898   hair
- 3740   medallion, robe
- 3032   clothing, cross
- 712 #12 pearl cotton   net pattern (beginning and ending at intersections to create diamond pattern)

Guinevere
- 611   crown, borders, hair, clothing, medallion
- 792   lettering
- 930   hairbands, earrings, medallion
- 640   face detail, shoulders
- 3032   clothing
- 712 #12 pearl cotton   net pattern (beginning and ending at intersections to create diamond pattern)

sword block
- 611   blue "W" block, sword
- 791   lettering
- 317   sword
- 3045   crowns, border
- 3828   border

twisted vine border
- 611   border

Camelot nameplate, date, and initials
- 611   borders
- 792   lettering, numbers

castle medallion
- 611   border
- 3363   trees
- 413   roofs, windows
- 317   stonework, chimneys
- 3362   trees

striped background
- 712 #12 pearl cotton   vertical Backstitch

Lazy Daisy Stitch

- ⎡522   leaves
- ⎣3363
- ⎡3362   leaves
- ⎣3363

Specialty Stitch

- □ 712 #12 pearl cotton   Four-Sided Stitch
- ▽ 712 #12 pearl cotton   Three-Sided Stitch
- ✳ 422   Eyelet Stitch
- ⋀⋀ 712 #12 pearl cotton   Herringbone Stitch

Mill Hill Petite Glass Seed Beads

- ✳ 40557   gold

Attach beads with 1 strand of DMC ecru.
Add beads after all other stitching is complete.

DMC Pearl Cotton

- 712   #12 cream

We recommend working the design in the following order:
1. All Cross Stitches worked over 2 fabric threads.
2. All Cross Stitches worked over 1 fabric thread.
3. All Backstitches.
4. All Specialty Stitches and beads.

The chart is divided into 13 sections.
Use the following diagram for placement.

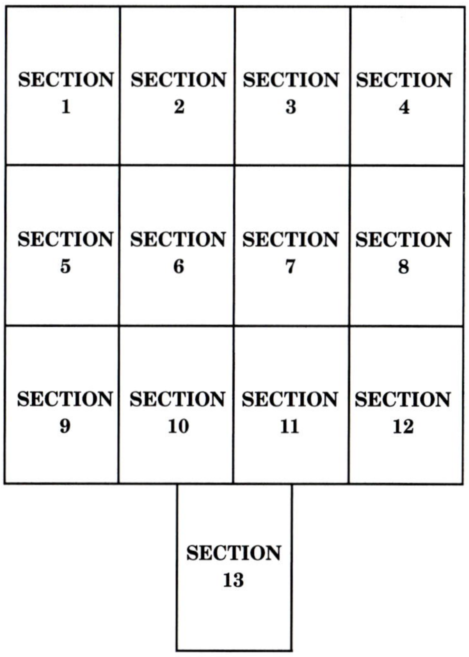

SECTION 1	SECTION 2	SECTION 3	SECTION 4
SECTION 5	SECTION 6	SECTION 7	SECTION 8
SECTION 9	SECTION 10	SECTION 11	SECTION 12

	SECTION 13	

CHART SECTIONS PLACEMENT DIAGRAM

CAMELOT SAMPLER SECTION 1

AMELOT SAMPLER SECTION 2

Shaded row indicates overlap from Section 2.

CAMELOT SAMPLER SECTION 3

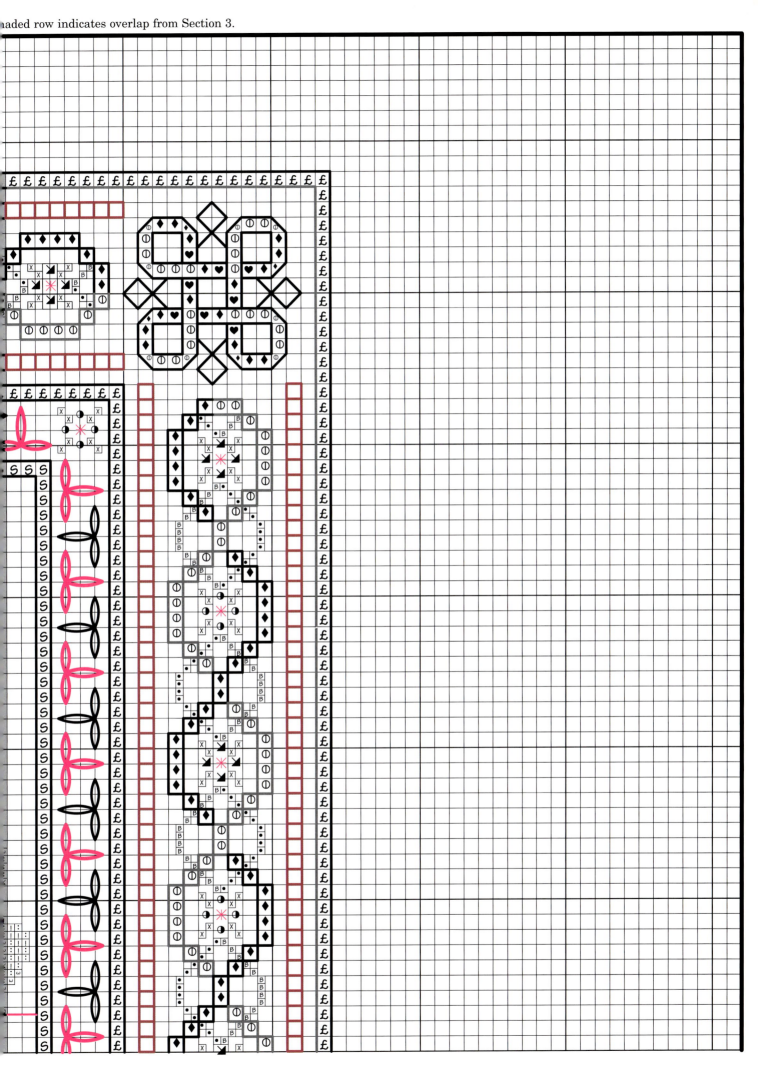

CAMELOT SAMPLER SECTION 4

Shaded row indicates overlap from Section 1.

CAMELOT SAMPLER SECTION 5

Shaded row indicates overlap from Sections 3 and 6.

CAMELOT SAMPLER SECTION 7

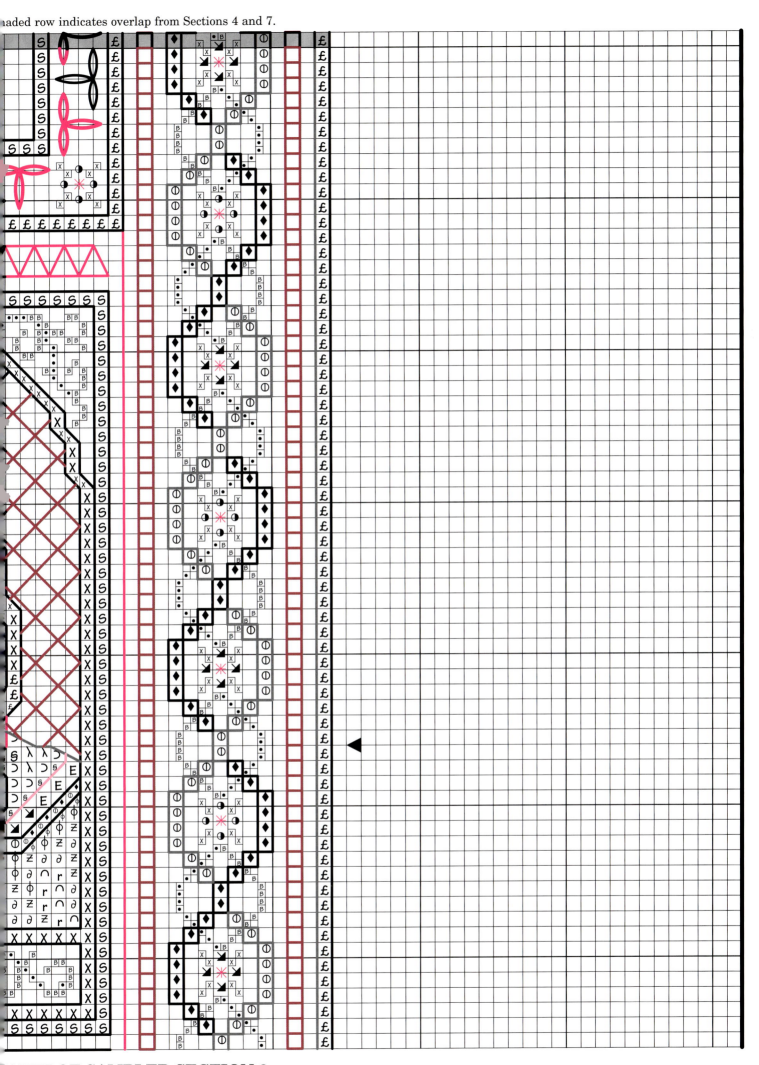

Shaded row indicates overlap from Section 5.

CAMELOT SAMPLER SECTION 9

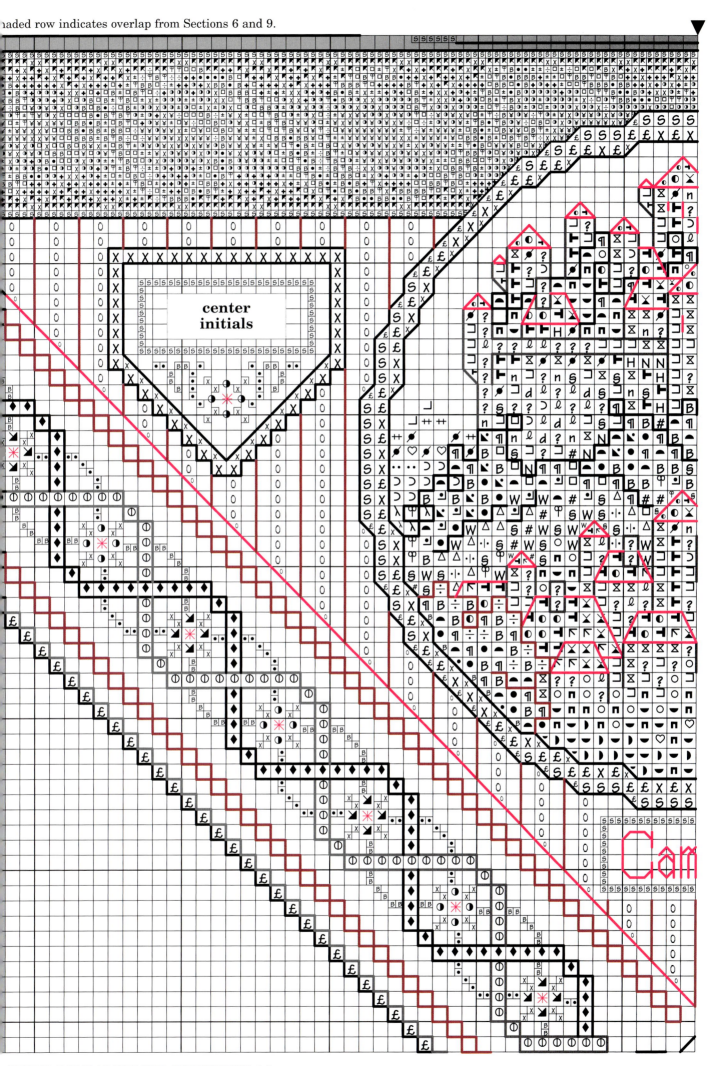

CAMELOT SAMPLER SECTION 10

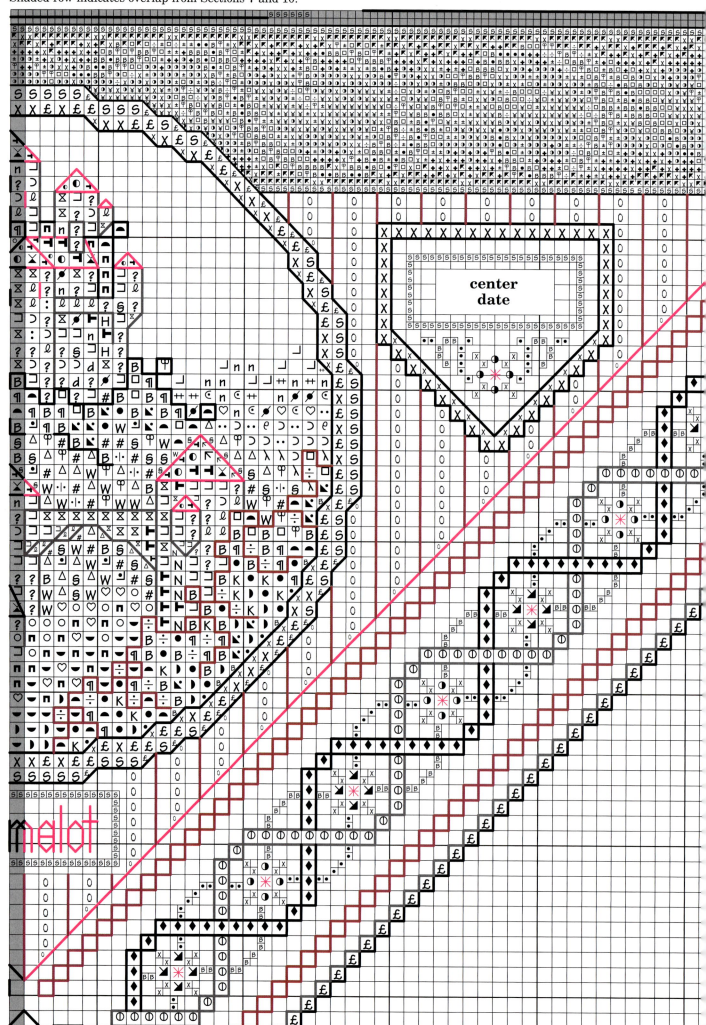

haded row indicates overlap from Section 8 and 11.

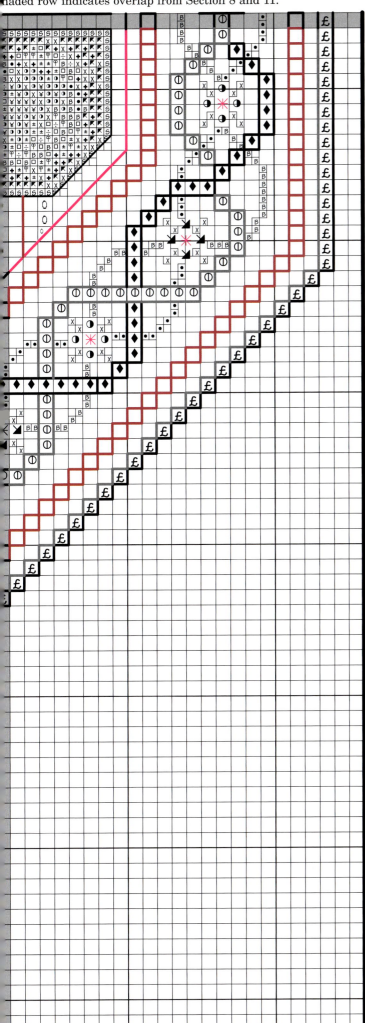
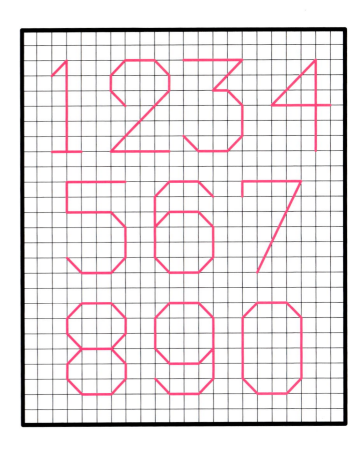

CAMELOT SAMPLER SECTION 12

43

Shaded row indicates overlap from Sections 10 and 11.

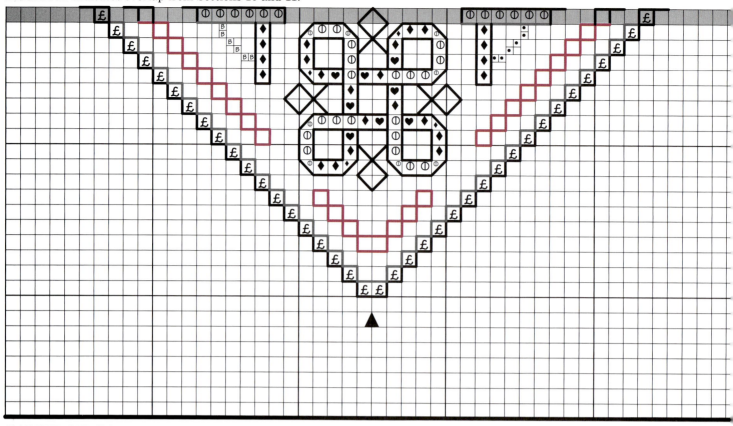

CAMELOT SAMPLER SECTION 13

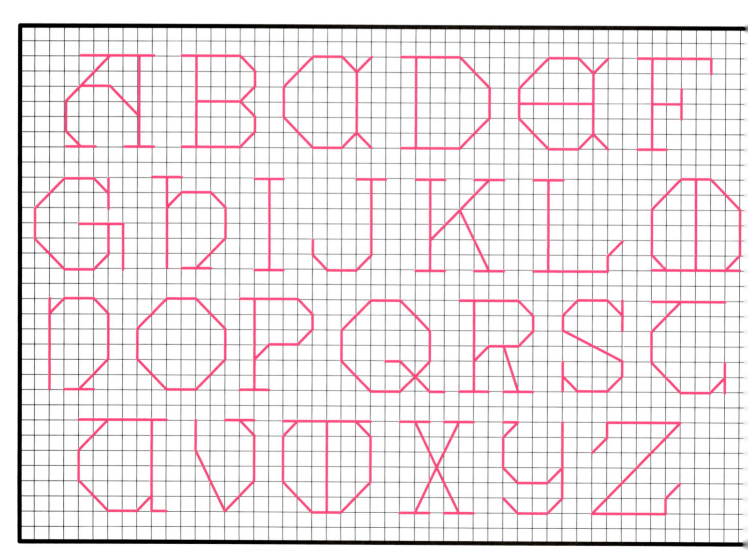

UPPER-CASE ALPHABET DETAIL

Fantasy Sampler

Our model was stitched over two fabric threads on 35 count Off White Linen from Norden Crafts, using 2 strands of floss for Cross Stitches, 1 strand of each color floss for Blended Cross Stitches and Blended Backstitches, and 1 strand for all other Backstitches and Lazy Daisy Stitches unless noted. Two sizes of alphabets are provided on page 49 for personalization.

Stitch Count: 174w x 234h
Design Size:
25 ct fabric (over 2 threads) 14" x 18¾"
28 ct fabric (over 2 threads) 12½" x 16¾"
32 ct fabric (over 2 threads) 10⅞" x 14⅝"

Cross Stitch

Symbol	DMC	COLOR
:	blanc / 712	white / cream
l	311	med navy blue
\	315	dk antique mauve
•	315 / 3041	dk antique mauve / med antique violet
e	316	med antique mauve
A	316 / 3042	med antique mauve / lt antique violet
P	316 / 3042 / 092	med antique mauve / lt antique violet / star pink metallic
B	318 / 451	lt steel grey / dk shell grey
O	341 / 932	lt periwinkle blue / lt antique blue
N	341 / 932 / 094	lt periwinkle blue / lt antique blue / star blue metallic
▽	341 / 3042	lt periwinkle blue / lt antique violet
U	415 / 452	pearl grey / med shell grey
X	420	dk hazelnut brown
∧	422	lt hazelnut brown
ψ	422 / 3045	lt hazelnut brown / dk yellow beige
6	434 / 840	lt brown / beige brown
−	435 / 841	vy lt brown / lt beige brown
△	437 / 842	lt tan / vy lt beige brown
/	453 / 762	lt shell grey / vy lt pearl grey

Cross Stitch

Symbol	DMC	COLOR
m	500	vy dk blue green
4	501 / 520	dk blue green / dk olive drab
3	522 / 3052	olive drab / med grey green
2	523 / 3053	med olive drab / grey green
·	524	lt olive drab
<	543 / 739	ultra vy lt beige brown / ultra vy lt tan
ø	610	vy dk drab brown
+	610 / 869	vy dk drab brown / vy dk hazelnut brown
#	610 / 3021	vy dk drab brown / dk brown grey
✱	611 / 612	dk drab brown / drab brown
C	738	vy lt tan
⊥	739	ultra vy lt tan
r	739 / 3042	ultra vy lt tan / lt antique violet
‖	754	lt peach flesh
⧺	754 / 841	lt peach flesh / lt beige brown
V	930	dk antique blue
=	931	med antique blue
↗	3021	dk brown grey
⊣	3041	med antique violet
,	3041 / 3042	med antique violet / lt antique violet
♥	3042	lt antique violet
W	3042 / 023	lt antique violet (**2 strands**) / lilac metallic (**1 strand**)
∩	3362 / 3363	dk loden green / loden green

Stitch the grey shaded areas as follows:
For C symbol, stitch the bottom leg of the Cross Stitch using the symbol shown in the chart. Then use 738/102c blend to finish crossing those stitches.
For ∧ symbol, stitch a full Cross Stitch using the symbol shown in the chart. Then stitch a full Cross Stitch over that with 102c (**1 strand**).

Backstitch
Backstitch in the following order:

	DMC	
∕	311	alphabet, upper and lower edges of the heart border
∕	317	unicorn and Pegasus
∕	420	hearts
∕	501	trees, floral border
∕	610	dragon, tree trunk, girl's hands, foot, and hair
∕	801	griffin and lion
∕	102c	dragon's tail detail and diamond detail (long stitches beginning from center and radiating out)
∕	500	central tree
∕	931	dress
∕	315 / 3041	dragon's tail (**1 strand each**)
∕	3041	flowers in border, hearts
∕	840	girl's face
∕	3021	dragon's feet, tree trunks, and instrument

Lazy Daisy
O 315
O 316

Kreinik Metallic Threads
#023 lilac blending filament
#092 star pink blending filament
#094 star blue blending filament
#102c Vatican gold cord

FANTASY SAMPLER SECTION 1

Shaded row indicates overlap from Section 1.

FANTASY SAMPLER SECTION 3

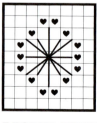

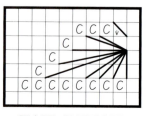

DIAMOND DETAIL   **TAIL DETAIL**

haded rows indicate overlap from Sections 2 and 3.

ANTASY SAMPLER SECTION 4

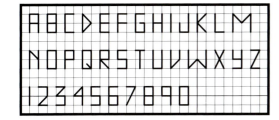

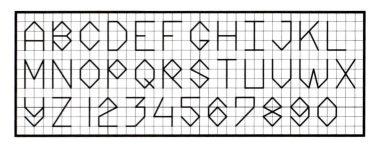

English Cottage Sampler

Our model was stitched over two fabric threads on 25 count Driftwood Linen by Zweigart®, using 2 strands of floss for Cross Stitches, French Knots, Lazy Daisy Stitches, and all Specialty Stitches, 1 strand of each color floss for Blended Cross Stitches, and 1 strand for Backstitches unless noted.

Stitch Count: 200w x 300h
Design Size:
25 ct fabric (over 2 threads) 16" x 24"
28 ct fabric (over 2 threads) 14⅜" x 21½"
32 ct fabric (over 2 threads) 12½" x 18¾"

Cross Stitch

Symbol	DMC	COLOR
·	blanc	white
	224	lt shell pink
B	778	lt antique mauve
3	316	med antique mauve
A	316	med antique mauve
	3041	med antique violet
#	317	pewter grey
↘	356	med terra cotta
	611	dk drab brown
H	369	vy lt pistachio green
	504	lt blue green
●	413	dk pewter grey
⊟	414	dk steel grey
Z	422	lt hazelnut brown
	437	lt tan
∪	422	lt hazelnut brown
	739	ultra vy lt tan
h	451	dk shell grey
M	451	dk shell grey
	927	med grey blue
★	451	dk shell grey
	3042	lt antique violet
÷	452	med shell grey
	453	lt shell grey
F	452	med shell grey
	3042	lt antique violet
:	453	lt shell grey
e	453	lt shell grey
	928	lt grey blue
X	500	vy dk blue green
L	501	dk blue green
ø	501	dk blue green
	520	dk olive drab
K	502	blue green
<	502	blue green
	522	olive drab
8	502	blue green
	932	lt antique blue
4	503	med blue green
▽	503	med blue green
	504	lt blue green
⊥	503	med blue green
	523	med olive drab
‖	504	lt blue green
∧	610	vy dk drab brown
	645	vy dk beaver grey

Cross Stitch

Symbol	DMC	COLOR
a	610	vy dk drab brown
	919	red copper
+	611	dk drab brown
	646	dk beaver grey
r	612	med drab brown
	647	med beaver grey
P	613	lt drab brown
d	762	vy lt pearl grey
c	775	lt baby blue
	932	lt antique blue
ε	778	lt antique mauve
	3042	lt antique violet
6	841	lt beige brown
	842	vy lt beige brown
◣	922	lt copper
=	930	dk antique blue
N	930	dk antique blue
	931	med antique blue
I	931	med antique blue
o	931	med antique blue
	932	lt antique blue
s	932	lt antique blue
t	3041	med antique violet
	3042	lt antique violet

Backstitch

Backstitch in the following order:

DMC	Description
311	blue border
317	cottage walls, chimneys, and porch pillars
413	window panes
500	green border, stems and leaves of floral border
610	roof
931 / 932	initials and date for personalizing
3041	medallions
930	blue borders, water around swans, blue alphabets (**2** strands for lower case alphabet)
3021	outer edges of roofs
839	gold borders, swans
3799	window frames and bases of chimneys
315	flowers in floral border, Roman numerals, hearts in swan border, and mauve alphabet
501	green border and shrubbery
414	swans and border above Roman numerals

French Knot
  414 eyes

Lazy Daisy
  501 leaves
  502 leaves

Specialty Stitches
  blanc Algerian Eye Stitch
  [224
   778] Algerian Eye Stitch
  [422
   437] Algerian Eye Stitch
  316 Scotch Stitch
  613 Alternating Scotch Stitch
  [612
   647] Large Smyrna Cross Stitch

Mill Hill Glass Seed Beads
  00168 blue
  00206 mauve
  00479 white

Attach blue beads with **1** strand of DMC 931.
Attach mauve beads with **1** strand of DMC 316.
Attach white beads with **1** strand of DMC blanc.
Add beads after all other stitching is complete.

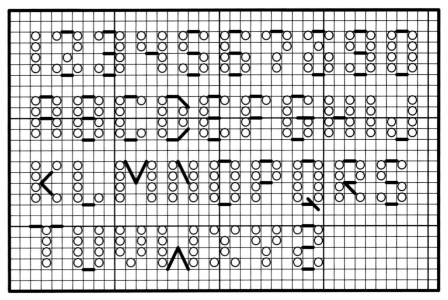

Note: Personalize sampler with **1** strand each med antique blue and lt antique blue using numbers and alphabet provided.

The chart is divided into eight sections. Use the following diagram for placement.

SECTION 5	SECTION 6	SECTION 7	SECTION 8
SECTION 1	SECTION 2	SECTION 3	SECTION 4

CHART SECTIONS PLACEMENT DIAGRAM

ENGLISH COTTAGE SAMPLER SECTION 1

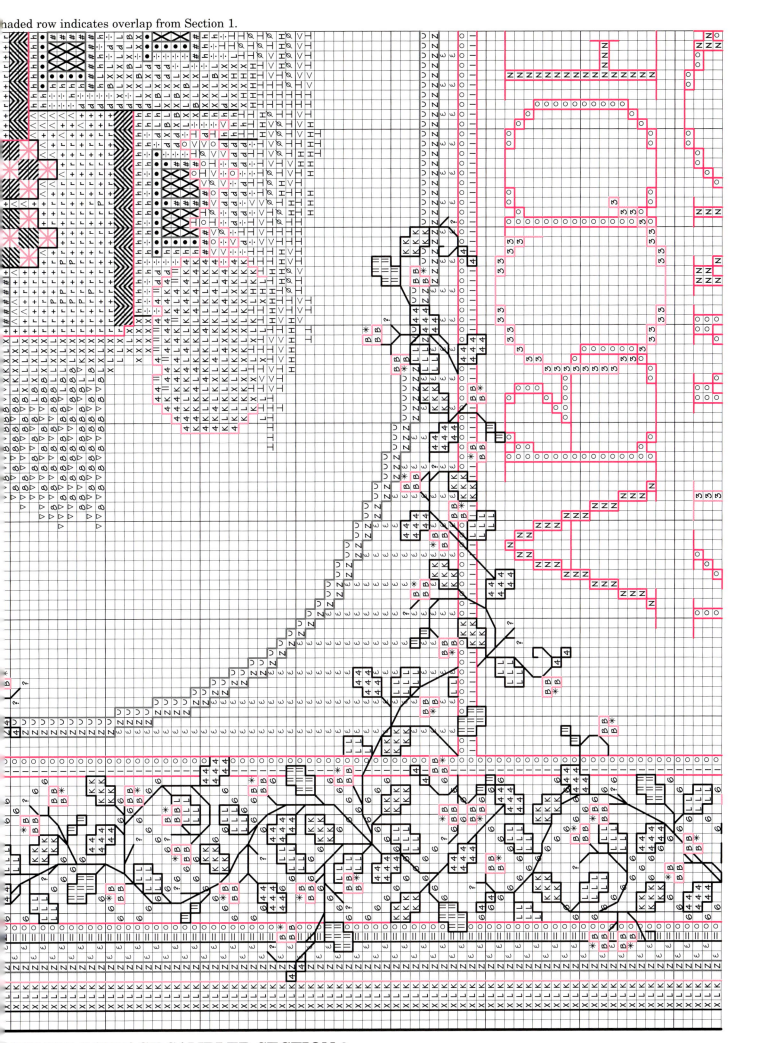

ENGLISH COTTAGE SAMPLER SECTION 2

ENGLISH COTTAGE SAMPLER SECTION 3

Shaded row indicates overlap from Section 1.

ENGLISH COTTAGE SAMPLER SECTION 5

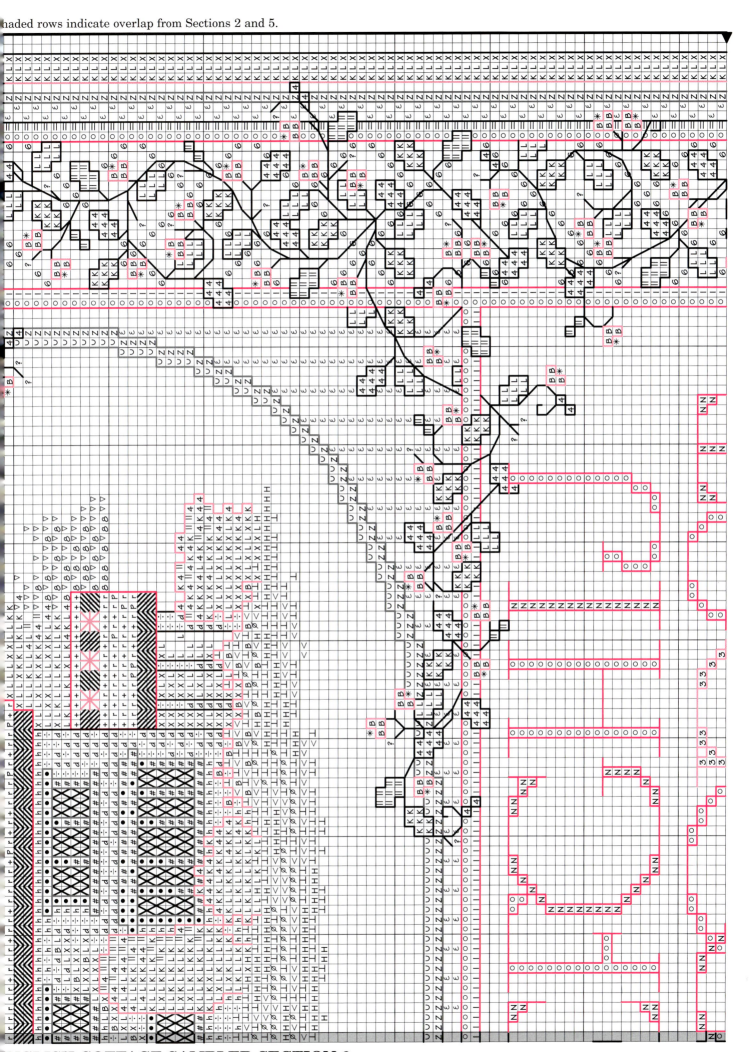

Shaded rows indicate overlap from Sections 3 and 6.

ENGLISH COTTAGE SAMPLER SECTION 7

ENGLISH COTTAGE SAMPLER SECTION 8

English Garden Sampler

Our model was stitched over two fabric threads on 25 count Antique White Lugana fabric from Zweigart®, using 2 strands of floss for Cross Stitches and 1 strand for Backstitches unless noted. For all Blended Stitches, refer to color key for number of strands used. Use 1 strand of floss for Cross Stitches worked over one fabric thread. *Because of the Cross Stitches worked over one fabric thread, this design is not suitable for Aida fabric. We recommend stitching the design in the order listed.*

Stitch Count: 194w x 272h
Design Size: 25 ct fabric (over 2 threads) 15⅝" x 21⅞"
28 ct fabric (over 2 threads) 13⅞" x 19½"
32 ct fabric (over 2 threads) 12⅛" x 17"

Cross Stitch

Symbol	DMC	COLOR
•	blanc	white
y *⌈	blanc	white
⌊	928	lt grey blue
♥ *⌈	315	dk antique mauve
⌊	3740	dk antique violet
¶ *⌈	316	med antique mauve
⌊	3042	lt antique violet
	317	pewter grey
≠	318	lt steel grey
◇ *⌈	318	lt steel grey
⌊	927	med grey blue
A *⌈	318	lt steel grey
⌊	3042	lt antique violet
∧ *⌈	318	lt steel grey
⌊	3743	vy lt antique violet
◖	319	vy dk pistachio green
W *⌈	340	periwinkle blue
⌊	3041	med antique violet
¢ *⌈	341	lt periwinkle blue
⌊	3042	lt antique violet
++ *⌈	371	pecan
⌊	3045	dk yellow beige
∴ *⌈	372	lt pecan
⌊	422	lt hazelnut brown
f	414	dk steel grey
? *⌈	414	dk steel grey
⌊	926	dk grey blue
6 *⌈	414	dk steel grey
⌊	3042	lt antique violet
⊖	415	pearl grey
¬ *⌈	415	pearl grey
⌊	524	lt olive drab
∽ *⌈	415	pearl grey
⌊	927	med grey blue
ø *⌈	415	pearl grey
⌊	3743	vy lt antique violet
▲	420	dk hazelnut brown
↗ *⌈	420	dk hazelnut brown
⌊	3011	dk khaki green
X	422	lt hazelnut brown
g *⌈	422	lt hazelnut brown
⌊	739	ul vy lt tan
∈ *⌈	422	lt hazelnut brown
⌊	3013	lt khaki green
*⌈	422	lt hazelnut brown
÷ ⌊	3013	lt khaki green
⌊	085	peacock metallic
2 *⌈	422	lt hazelnut brown
⌊	3045	dk yellow beige
N *⌈	422	lt hazelnut brown
⌊	3046	med yellow beige
@ *⌈	434	lt brown
⌊	3790	ul dk beige grey

Cross Stitch

Symbol	DMC	COLOR
△ *⌈	435	vy lt brown
⌊	840	med beige brown
■	500	vy dk blue green
★ *⌈	500	vy dk blue green
⌊	520	dk olive drab
● *⌈	500	vy dk blue green
⌊	924	vy dk grey blue
○	501	dk blue green
↘ *⌈	501	dk blue green
⌊	3362	dk loden green
£ *⌈	501	dk blue green
⌊	3363	loden green
# *⌈	501	dk blue green
⌊	3768	dk grey green
K	502	blue green
o *⌈	502	blue green
⌊	522	olive drab
z *⌈	502	blue green
⌊	926	dk grey blue
·|· *⌈	502	blue green
⌊	3363	loden green
||	503	med blue green
♪ *⌈	503	med blue green
⌊	523	med olive drab
μ	504	lt blue green
⊃ *⌈	504	lt blue green
⌊	524	lt olive drab
▲	520	dk olive drab
f	522	olive drab
∞ *⌈	522	olive drab
⌊	3052	med grey green
B *⌈	522	olive drab
⌊	3363	loden green
⊥	523	med olive drab
\	524	lt olive drab
æ *⌈	543	ul vy lt beige brown
⌊	739	ul vy lt tan
R	561	dk sea foam green
ø *⌈	561	dk sea foam green
⌊	792	dk cornflower blue
▶ *⌈	561	dk sea foam green
⌊	3362	dk loden green
∪	562	sea foam green
*	562	sea foam green
□	793	med cornflower blue
⌊	085	peacock metallic
♭ *⌈	562	sea foam green
⌊	3363	loden green
♦ *⌈	611	dk drab brown
⌊	3045	dk yellow beige
«	640	vy dk beige grey
⊓	642	dk beige grey

Cross Stitch

Symbol	DMC	COLOR
*	738	vy lt tan
∨	3013	lt khaki green
⌊	085	peacock metallic
∴ *⌈	739	ul vy lt tan
⌊	3013	lt khaki green
>	762	vy lt pearl grey
⌐ *⌈	762	vy lt pearl grey
⌊	3743	vy lt antique violet
⊕ *⌈	778	lt antique mauve
⌊	3743	vy lt antique violet
▼	791	vy dk cornflower blue
⊙ *⌈	791	vy dk cornflower blue
⌊	3740	dk antique violet
&	792	dk cornflower blue
ε *⌈	792	dk cornflower blue
⌊	3041	med antique violet
↗ *⌈	792	dk cornflower blue
⌊	3362	dk loden green
b *⌈	793	med cornflower blue
⌊	3363	loden green
◁ †⌈	793	med cornflower blue
⌊	085	peacock metallic
e	794	lt cornflower blue
●	934	black avocado green
	991	dk aquamarine
κ	3011	dk khaki green
↖ *⌈	3011	dk khaki green
⌊	3051	dk grey green
✳ *⌈	3011	dk khaki green
⌊	3362	dk loden green
$	3012	med khaki green
§ *⌈	3012	med khaki green
⌊	3045	dk yellow beige
: *⌈	3012	med khaki green
⌊	3052	med grey green
⊐	3013	lt khaki green
// *⌈	3013	lt khaki green
⌊	3053	grey green
⊖	3041	med antique violet
M *⌈	3041	med antique violet
⌊	3726	dk antique mauve
∇	3042	lt antique violet
ꙅ	3045	dk yellow beige
⦿	3051	dk grey green
⊠	3052	med grey green
ω	3053	grey green
8	3362	dk loden green
⊙	3363	loden green
<	3364	lt loden green
	3787	dk brown grey
⊼	3790	ul dk beige grey

* Use 1 strand of each color listed.
† Use 2 strands of first color listed and 1 strand of second color listed.

DMC Pearl Cotton
ecru #12

Kreinik Metallic Threads
085 peacock blending filament

Mill Hill Glass Seed Beads
  00020 royal blue
  00151 ash mauve
  00206 violet
  00252 iris
  02001 pearl
  02005 dusty rose

Attach royal blue, violet and iris beads using 1 strand DMC 3041.
Attach ash mauve and dusty rose beads using 1 strand DMC 3042.
Attach pearl beads using 1 strand DMC 739.
Add beads after all other stitching is complete.

Outer Border
Corner Medallions
1. Work Cross Stitch.
2. *[341 / 3042]   Satin Stitch
3. *[341 / 3042]   Medium Diamond Eyelet Stitch
4. 3041
5. *[543 / 739]   Eight-Sided Eyelet Stitch
6. 3740
7. 520
8. 3787

Border Strips
1. Work Cross Stitch.
2. *[341 / 3042]   Eight-Sided Eyelet Stitch
3. 3740
4. *[543 / 739]   Eyelet Variation Stitch
5. 3045
6. 420   net pattern (long stitches)
7. 102c   Upright Cross
8. 3041   net pattern border
9. 3787   outer edges of border

Fountain Scene and Peacocks
1. Work Cross Stitch.
   520   greenery
   3363   greenery
   317   pillars, steps, and fountain
   *[502 / 3363]   Alternating Scotch Stitch
   *[501 / 3362]   Alternating Scotch Stitch
   3362   border
   791   peacocks (**1** strand for bottom peacock and **2** strands for top peacock)
   3051   tails
10. 3787   feet, legs, wings, eyes, and beaks (**1** strand for bottom peacock and **2** strands for top peacock)
11. 422   Satin Stitch
12. Work Cross Stitch over one thread, section above Satin Stitch on top knot peacock using DMC 791.
13. *[562 / 991]   tails

Border Under Fountain Scene
1. Work Cross Stitch.
2. *[422 / 543 / 739]   Satin Stitch
3. *[522 / 3363]   Lazy Daisy Stitch
4. 102c   (long stitches)
5. 3787   border

Alphabet and Gate
1. Work Cross Stitch over one thread. *Backstitch on main chart is for placement purposes only.*
2. 317   Gate

Border Above and Below Alphabet
1. *[543 / 739]   Eyelet Variation Stitch
2. *[522 / 3363]   Lazy Daisy Stitch

Topiary Blocks
1. Work Cross Stitch.
2. 520   greenery
3. 317   urns
4. 3790   topiary trunks, corner blocks
5. *[543 / 739]   Eight-Sided Eyelet Stitch
6. 3740   borders, Eight-Sided Eyelet Stitch
7. 422   net pattern

Whitework Border
1. *[422 / 543 / 739]   Satin Stitch
2. ecru #12 Satin Stitch
3. ecru #12 Large Diamond Eyelet
4. *[422 / 739]   Lazy Daisy Stitch
5. ecru #12
6. Wrap ecru #12 using 102c.

Numeral Border
1. Work Cross Stitch.
2. *[522 / 3363]   Alternating Scotch Stitch
3. *[502 / 3363]   Alternating Scotch Stitch
4. *[341 / 3042]   Medium Diamond Eyelet Stitch
5. *[316 / 3042]   Medium Diamond Eyelet Stitch
6. 3041
7. *[611 / 3045]   numbers
8. *[422 / 739]   Herringbone Stitch

Cutwork Border
1. *[341 / 3042]   Eight-Sided Eyelet Stitch
2. 3740
3. ecru #12 Satin Stitch
4. ecru #12 pearl cotton Hemstitch both edges of cutwork areas on all four sides of sampler.
5. Using small, pointed scissors, carefully cut 8 vertical threads when working on the vertical columns of border. Cut 8 horizontal threads when working on the horizontal columns of border. Remove cut threads without pulling fabric out of shape.
6. Using ecru #12 pearl cotton, anchor pearl cotton behind work at center of one of the Satin Stitch bars. Knot three pairs of threads together, working across the row. Anchor pearl cotton at the end of the row.
Note: To be sure you cut the #12 pearl cotton long enough to complete knotting the clusters for the whole row, double the length of the area you are stitching.

CHARTS SECTIONS PLACEMENT DIAGRAM
The chart is divided into nine sections.
Use the following diagram for placement.

SECTION 1	SECTION 2	SECTION 3
SECTION 4	SECTION 5	SECTION 6
SECTION 7	SECTION 8	SECTION 9

ENGLISH GARDEN SAMPLER SECTION 1

Shaded rows indicate overlap from Section 1.

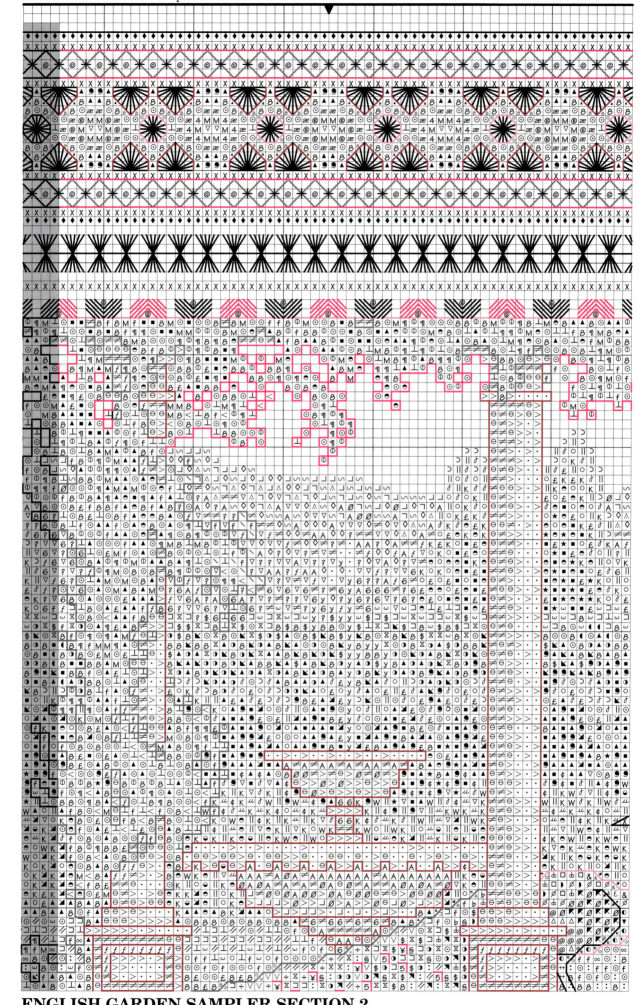

ENGLISH GARDEN SAMPLER SECTION 2

Shaded rows indicate overlap from Section 2.

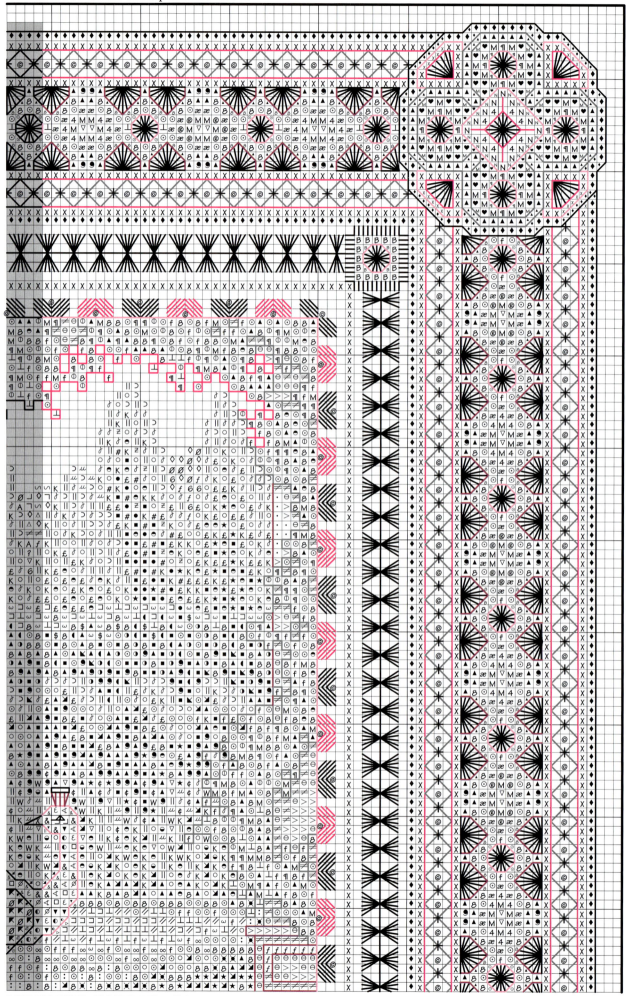

ENGLISH GARDEN SAMPLER SECTION 3

Shaded rows indicate overlap from Section 1.

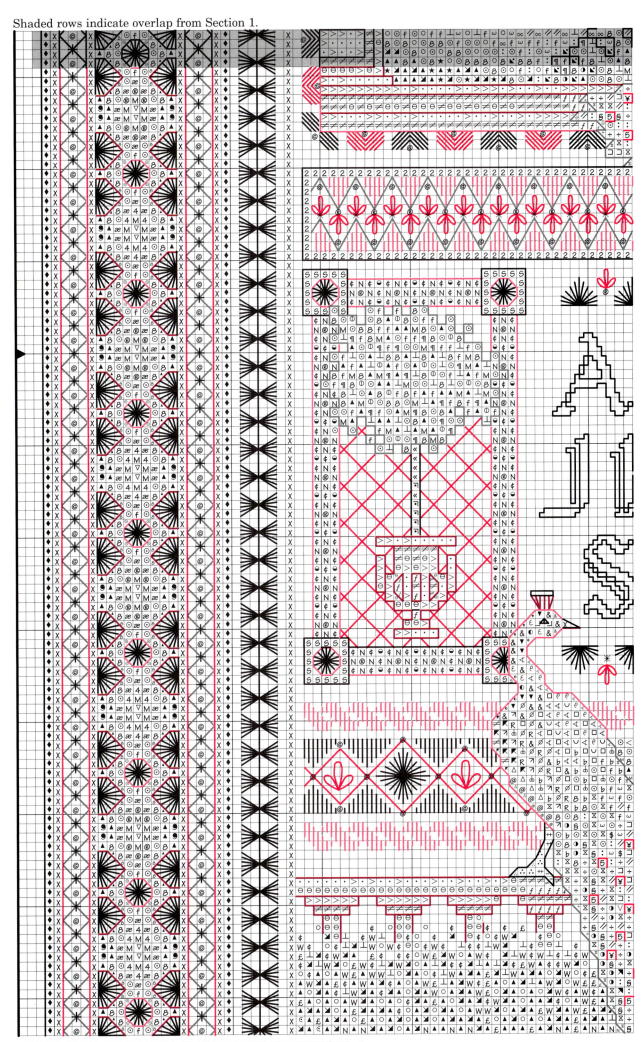

ENGLISH GARDEN SAMPLER SECTION 4

Shaded rows indicate overlaps from Sections 2 and 4.

ENGLISH GARDEN SAMPLER SECTION 5

Shaded rows indicate overlaps from Sections 3 and 5.

ENGLISH GARDEN SAMPLER SECTION 6

Shaded rows indicate overlap from Section 4.

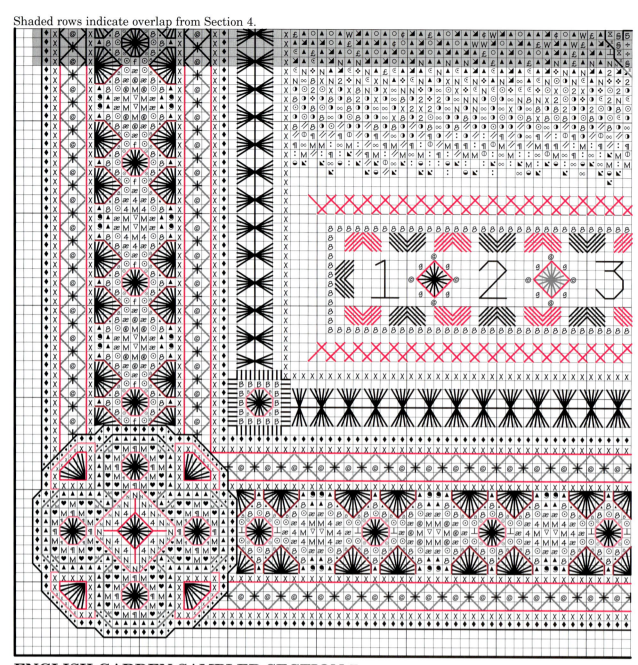

ENGLISH GARDEN SAMPLER SECTION 7

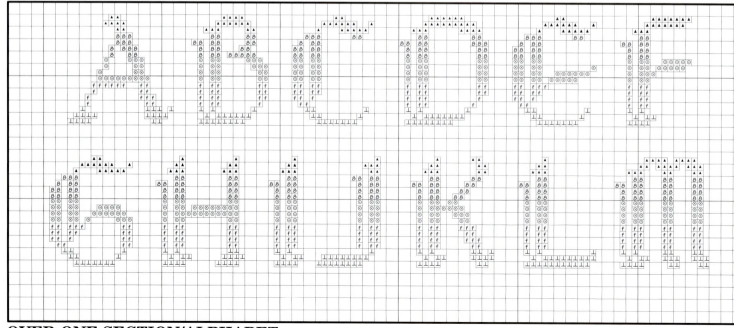

OVER-ONE SECTION/ALPHABET

Shaded rows indicate overlaps from Sections 5 and 7.

ENGLISH GARDEN SAMPLER SECTION 8

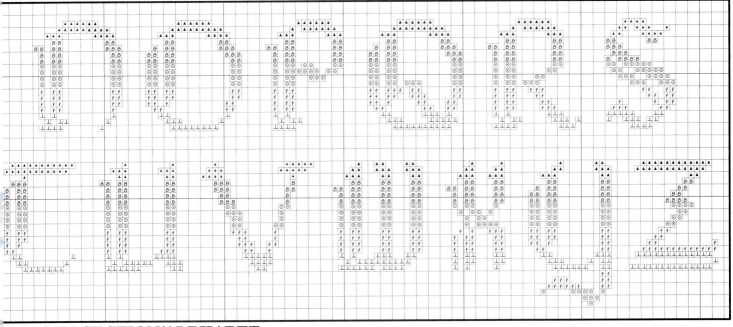

VER-ONE SECTION/ALPHABET

Shaded rows indicate overlaps from Sections 6 and 8.

ENGLISH GARDEN SAMPLER SECTION 9

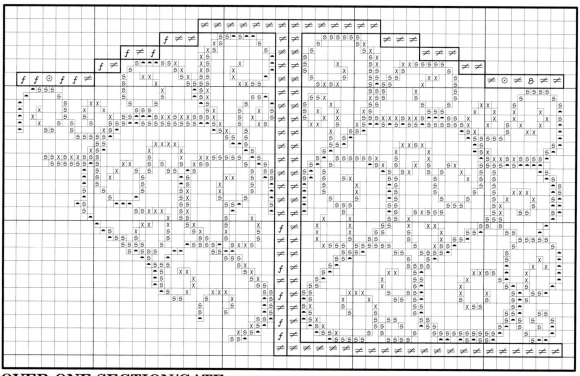

OVER-ONE SECTION/GATE

Birth Announcement

ur model was stitched over two fabric threads on 28 count Ivory Monaco fabric from Charles Craft, Inc., sing 2 strands of floss for Cross Stitches, Half Cross Stitches, Lazy Daisy Stitches, and Specialty Stitches, strand of each color floss for all Blended Stitches, and 1 strand for Backstitches unless noted. Use 1 strand f floss for Cross Stitches and Backstitches worked over one fabric thread. *Because of the Cross Stitches nd Backstitches worked over one fabric thread, this design is not suitable for Aida fabric.* Complete all ross Stitches, Specialty Stitches, then Backstitches. Alphabets and numbers are provided for ersonalization. Backstitch for areas stitched over one thread is shown on the main chart for placement ly. Refer to alphabet chart, pg. 75, for actual Backstitch.

Stitch Count: 176w x 191h
Design Size: 25 ct fabric (over 2 threads) 14½" x 15⅜"
28 ct fabric (over 2 threads) 12⅝" x 13¾"
32 ct fabric (over 2 threads) 11" x 12"

ross Stitch

DMC	COLOR
ecru	ecru
ecru	ecru
3033	lt brown grey
316	med antique mauve
3041	med antique violet
320	med pistachio green
522	olive drab
320	med pistachio green
3045	dk yellow beige
340	periwinkle blue
340	periwinkle blue
3041	med antique violet
341	lt periwinkle blue
341	lt periwinkle blue
3042	lt antique violet
368	lt pistachio green
422	lt hazelnut brown
368	lt pistachio green
523	med olive drab
369	vy lt pistachio green
524	lt olive drab
369	vy lt pistachio green
738	vy lt tan
420	dk hazelnut brown
611	dk drab brown
420	dk hazelnut brown
680	dk old gold
422	lt hazelnut brown
676	lt old gold
422	lt hazelnut brown
3042	lt antique violet
422	lt hazelnut brown
3782	lt mocha brown
452	med shell grey
452	med shell grey
3042	lt antique violet
452	med shell grey
3782	lt mocha brown
453	lt shell grey
453	lt shell grey
762	vy lt pearl grey
453	lt shell grey
842	vy lt beige brown
453	lt shell grey
3743	vy lt antique violet
502	blue green
502	blue green
522	olive drab
503	med blue green
503	med blue green
523	med olive drab
504	lt blue green
504	lt blue green
524	lt olive drab

Cross Stitch

	DMC	COLOR
5	522	olive drab
t	523	med olive drab
b	524	lt olive drab
c	543	ul vy lt beige brown
	739	ul vy lt tan
◐	610	vy dk drab brown
⌀	611	dk drab brown
⚹	611	dk drab brown
	612	med drab brown
r	612	med drab brown
=	677	vy lt old gold
	738	vy lt tan
⊙	729	med old gold
	3045	dk yellow beige
2	738	vy lt tan
	842	vy lt beige brown
ℓ	738	vy lt tan
	3743	vy lt antique violet
‥	739	ul vy lt tan
	3823	ul pale yellow
∕	746	off white
ε	778	lt antique mauve
~	778	lt antique mauve
	3743	vy lt antique violet
A	841	lt beige brown
	3042	lt antique violet
♡	950	lt coco brown
?	3013	lt khaki green
⊗	3032	med mocha brown
	3045	dk yellow beige
⊼	3033	vy lt mocha brown
	3782	lt mocha brown
8	3041	med antique violet
	3042	lt antique violet
«	3042	lt antique violet
∪	3042	lt antique violet
	3727	lt antique mauve
φ	3042	lt antique violet
	3743	vy lt antique violet
▲	3362	dk loden green
E	3363	loden green
V	3743	vy lt antique violet
∩	3743	vy lt antique violet
	3747	vy lt blue violet
↘	3747	vy lt blue violet
:	3770	vy lt flesh
∂	3774	vy lt sportsman flesh

Stitch the grey shaded areas as follows: Stitch the bottom leg of the Cross Stitch using the symbol shown in the chart. Then use one strand of 762 to finish crossing those stitches.

Half Cross Stitch

	DMC	COLOR
ω	369	vy lt pistachio green
£	523	med olive drab
9	524	lt olive drab

Backstitch

	DMC	COLOR
∕	340	alphabets, numbers
∕	610	left angel's hair
∕	3363	stems, edges of greenery against fabric
∕	611	all other
∕	ecru	rope (**3** strands)

Note: Use **1** strand 422 for Wrapped Backstitch on rope.

	DMC	COLOR
∕	316	lips
∕	3045	Square Eyelets, Diamond Eyelets
∕	451	all other
∕	612	net pattern
∕	841	wings, flesh
∕	3362	edges of greenery in foreground
∕	501	remaining greenery
∕	3041	violet on robes
∕	002	net pattern (long stitches)
∕	3032	diamond shapes, robes

Lazy Daisy

	DMC	COLOR
∅	368 / 422	leaf clusters
∅	522	leaves (**2** strands)
∅	523	leaves (**2** strands)

Specialty Stitch

	DMC	COLOR
✱	ecru	Medium and Large Diamond Eyelet Stitch
✵	ecru	Medium and Large Eyelet Stitch
+	3045	Upright Cross Stitch

Kreinik Metallic Threads
#002 gold blending filament

Mill Hill Petite Glass Seed Beads

	DMC	COLOR
✕	40123	cream
♥	40252	iris
✳	40557	gold
✚	42024	heather mauve

Attach beads using 1 strand DMC ecru. Add beads after all other stitching is complete.

BIRTH ANNOUNCEMENT SECTION 1

Shaded row indicates overlap from Section 1.

BIRTH ANNOUNCEMENT SECTION 3

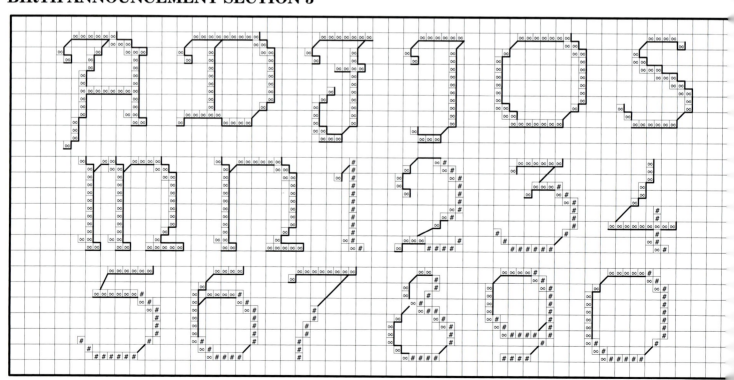

ALPHABET AND NUMBERS/OVER-ONE DETAIL
Note: Includes letters needed for months and "born" only.

74

BIRTH ANNOUNCEMENT SECTION 4

ALPHABET/OVER-ONE DETAIL
Note: Includes letters needed for months and "born" only.

ALPHABET/OVER-ONE DETAIL

ALPHABET/OVER-ONE DETAIL

Christmas Sampler

Our model was stitched over two fabric threads on 25 count Antique White Lugana fabric from Zweigart using 2 strands of floss for Cross Stitches, Half Cross Stitches, Lazy Daisy Stitches, and Specialty Stitches, 1 strand of each color floss for all Blended Stitches, and 1 strand for Backstitches unless noted. Use 1 strand of floss for Cross Stitches and Backstitches worked over one fabric thread. *Because of the Cross Stitches worked over one fabric thread, this design is not suitable for Aida fabric.* Complete all Cross Stitch in each area before beginning Specialty Stitches. *We recommend stitching the design in the order listed.*

Stitch Count: 124w x 152h
Design Size: 25 ct fabric (over 2 threads) 10" x 12¼"
  28 ct fabric (over 2 threads) 8⅞" x 10⅞"
  32 ct fabric (over 2 threads) 7¾" x 9½"

Cross Stitch

Symbol	DMC	COLOR
X	ecru	ecru
▲	315	dk antique mauve
◄	316	med antique mauve
⊞	[340 / 793]	periwinkle blue / med cornflower blue
7	[341 / 794]	lt periwinkle blue / lt cornflower blue
▼	413	dk pewter grey
◀	420	dk hazelnut brown
△	422	lt hazelnut brown
6	[422 / 3045]	lt hazelnut brown / dk yellow beige
⊃	[422 / 3046]	lt hazelnut brown / med yellow beige
⊗	434	lt brown
8	[434 / 435]	lt brown / vy lt brown
¥	435	vy lt brown
∞	436	tan
⊿	437	lt tan
⊥	501	dk blue green
@	[501 / 3362]	dk blue green / dk loden green
Æ	[501 / 3363]	dk blue green / loden green
S	502	blue green
N	[502 / 522]	blue green / olive drab
↓	[502 / 3363]	blue green / loden green
r	503	med blue green
=	[503 / 523]	med blue green / med olive drab
⌐	[504 / 524]	lt blue green / lt olive drab
●	520	dk olive drab
·|·	522	olive drab
⊿	523	med olive drab
⋈	610	vy dk drab brown
&	611	dk drab brown
◌	[611 / 3045]	dk drab brown / dk yellow beige
◇	612	med drab brown
÷	738	vy lt tan

Cross Stitch

Symbol	DMC	COLOR
6	791	vy dk cornflower blue
✎	792	dk cornflower blue
#	[792 / 3746]	dk cornflower blue / dk blue violet
⊂	793	med cornflower blue
▲	838	vy dk beige brown
$	839	dk beige brown
−	840	med beige brown
±	841	lt beige brown
~	842	vy lt beige brown
■	934	black avocado green
◒	3031	vy dk mocha brown
♂	3033	vy lt mocha brown
▫	3041	med antique violet
A	[3041 / 3042]	med antique violet / lt antique violet
+	[3041 / 3740]	med antique violet / dk antique violet
ϕ	3042	lt antique violet
★	3045	dk yellow beige
L	3046	med yellow beige
I	[3046 / 3047]	med yellow beige / lt yellow beige
x	[3051 / 3052]	dk grey green / med grey green
⊕	3052	med grey green
⚥	3053	grey green
◐	3362	dk loden green
§	3363	loden green
✕	3726	antique mauve
⊐	3727	lt antique mauve
♥	3740	dk antique violet
··	3770	vy lt flesh
μ	3774	vy lt sportsman flesh
ƶ	3782	lt mocha brown
●	3799	vy dk pewter grey

Half Cross Stitch

Symbol	DMC	COLOR
✱	[318 / 415]	lt steel grey / pearl grey
3	415	pearl grey
M	[415 / 3042]	pearl grey / lt antique violet

Half Cross Stitch

Symbol	DMC	COLOR
♭	[415 / 3743]	pearl grey / vy lt antique violet
?	502	blue green
H	[502 / 926]	blue green / dk grey green
∽	503	med blue green
↙	[503 / 927]	med blue green / med grey blue
:	504	lt blue green
○	[504 / 928]	lt blue green / lt grey blue
/	762	vy lt pearl grey
»	927	med grey blue

Kreinik Metallic Threads
210 gold #8 fine braid

DMC Rayon Floss
30712   cream rayon

Mill Hill Glass Seed Beads
∩ 00123 cream
G 00557 old gold
⊚ 40123 cream (petite)
O 40557 gold (petite)
✱ 42012 royal plum (petite)
Attach cream and royal plum beads using 1 strand DMC ecru.
Attach old gold and gold beads using 1 strand DMC 611.
Add beads after all other stitching is complete.

Outer Border
1. Cross Stitch border.
2. ╱ 611
3. ╱ [422 / 3045]
4. Wrap 422/3045 Backstitch using 30712 (**1** strand).
5. ○ [501 / 3362] Lazy Daisy Stitch
6. ○ [502 / 3363] Lazy Daisy Stitch

Snowflakes/Garland
1. Cross Stitch garland.
2. ✹ 30712 Medium Eyelet Stitch (**1** strand)
3. ✦ ecru Small Diamond Eyelet Stitch
4. ✱ ecru Large Diamond Eyelet Stitch
5. ▨ ecru Scotch Stitch
6. × ecru off center Cross Stitch
7. ✶ ecru Small Eyelet Stitch
8. ✷ ecru Large Eyelet Stitch
9. ✸ ecru Diamond Eyelet Variation Stitch
10. ／ 30712

(For more control when Backstitching with rayon, stitch over one fabric thread instead of over two.)

11. ／ [422 / 3045]
12. Wrap 422/3045 Backstitch using 210 #8 fine braid (**1** strand).
13. ／ [422 / 3045] Lazy Daisy Stitch
14. ／ 210 #8 fine braid Lazy Daisy Stitch (**1** strand)

Knotted Clusters
1. ‖‖‖‖ ecru Satin Stitch
2. ····· ecru Hemstitch top and bottom rows (indicated by dotted lines)

Note: These next two steps for the Knotted Clusters section should be done after all other stitching on the sampler has been completed.

3. Using small, pointed scissors, carefully cut the ten threads that run crosswise in this area, cutting close to the Satin Stitch bars. Remove cut threads without pulling fabric out of shape.
4. Using ecru (**2** strands), anchor floss behind work at center of one of the Satin Stitch bars. Gather and knot three pairs of threads together, working across the row. Anchor floss at the end of the row.

Alphabet and Greenery
Note: Cross Stitch and Backstitch alphabet (pg. 83) over one fabric thread. Black lines on chart are for placement only. Cross Stitch and Backstitch greenery over two fabric threads.
1. ／ 420
2. ／ 3362
3. ／ 3726

Whitework Blocks
1. Cross Stitch block borders.
2. ✹ ecru Medium Diamond Eyelet Stitch
3. ○ ecru Lazy Daisy Stitch
4. ／ 30712
5. ／ 3045

Herringbone Stitch Border
⨯⨯⨯ ecru Herringbone Stitch

Chain Stitch Row
Begin in center of row.
∞∞ [422 / 3045] Chain Stitch

Rope Motif and Flower Border
1. Cross Stitch flowers.
2. ‖‖‖‖ ecru Satin Stitch
3. ○ 3363 Lazy Daisy Stitch (**2** strands)
4. ／ 422
5. ／ 3041
6. ／ 3045
7. ／ 3363 (**1** strand)
8. ／ 3726

Horse and Sleigh Scene
Backstitch in the following order:
1. Cross Stitch scene.
2. ／ 3799 sleigh runners
3. ／ 611 all other
4. ／ 315 clothes, hat
5. ／ 838 arches, pillars
6. ／ 791 horse's blanket
7. ／ 3362 tree
8. ／ [318 / 414] snow
9. ／ 501 blanket on girl's lap
10. ／ 3781 harness, bridle, horse's eye, girl's hair
11. ／ 3740 mittens, horse's blanket, blue of sleigh
12. ／ 433 horse
13. ／ 610 sleigh

Horse and Sleigh Detail
1. ／ 3045 sleigh (**2** strands)
2. Wrap 3045 Backstitch using 422 (**1** strand).
3. ／ [422 / 3045] harness, sleigh
4. Wrap 422/3045 Backstitch using 210 #8 fine braid (**1** strand).

Twisted Cluster Border
1. ‖‖‖‖ ecru Satin Stitch

Note: These next two steps for the Twisted Cluster Border section should be done after all other stitching on the sampler has been completed.
2. Using small, pointed scissors, carefully cut the 12 threads that run crosswise in this area, cutting close to the Satin Stitch bars. Remove cut threads without pulling fabric out of shape.
3. Using ecru (**2** strands), anchor floss behind work at center of one of the Satin Stitch bars. Twist groups of four threads, working across the row. Anchor floss at the end of the row.

Date and Initial
1. ✹ ecru Medium Diamond Eyelet Stitch
2. ／ 30712
3. ／ [422 / 3045] alphabet, numbers (charted below)

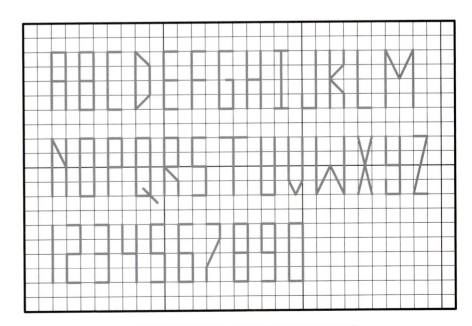

ALPHABET AND NUMBERS

79

CHRISTMAS SAMPLER SECTION 1

Shaded rows indicate overlap from Section 1.

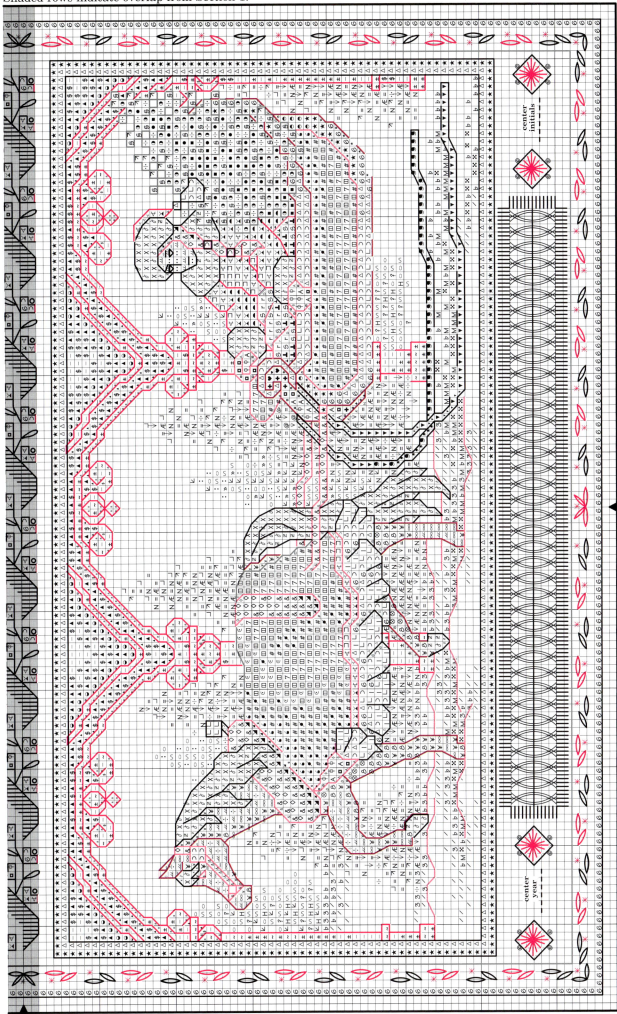

CHRISTMAS SAMPLER SECTION 2

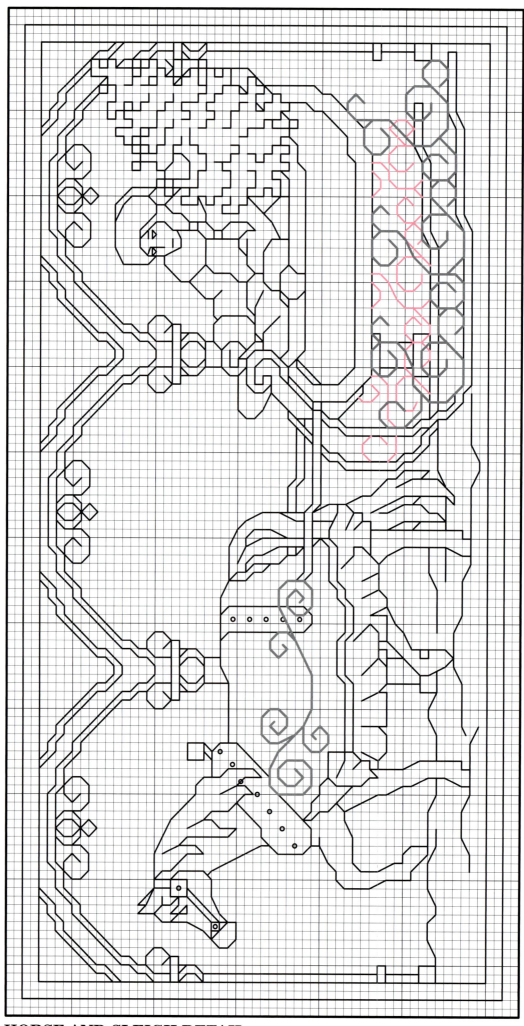

HORSE AND SLEIGH DETAIL (black lines are for placement only)

ALPHABET/OVER-ONE DETAIL

Wedding Sampler

Our model was stitched over two fabric threads on 32 count Platinum Belfast Linen from Zweigart®, using 2 strands of floss for Cross Stitches and Specialty Stitches, 1 strand of each color floss for all Blended Stitches, and 1 strand for Backstitches unless noted. Use 1 strand of floss for Cross Stitches and Backstitches worked over one fabric thread. *Because of the Cross Stitches and Backstitches worked over one fabric thread, this design is not suitable for Aida fabric.* Complete all Cross Stitches, Specialty Stitches, then Backstitches. Alphabets and numbers are provided for personalization. Backstitch for areas stitched over one thread is shown on the main chart for placement only. Refer to alphabet and number charts, pgs. 87-89, for actual Backstitch.

Stitch Count: 140w x 168h
Design Size:
- 25 ct fabric (over 2 threads) 11¼" x 13½"
- 28 ct fabric (over 2 threads) 10" x 12"
- 32 ct fabric (over 2 threads) 8¾" x 10½"

Cross Stitch

DMC	COLOR
blanc	white
ecru	ecru
315 / 3740	dk antique mauve / dk antique violet
316 / 3042	med antique mauve / lt antique violet
340 / 931	periwinkle blue / med antique blue
341 / 932	lt periwinkle blue / lt antique blue
422	lt hazelnut brown
422 / 3045	lt hazelnut brown / dk yellow beige
422 / 3046	lt hazelnut brown / med yellow beige
452	med shell grey
452 / 3032	med shell grey / med mocha brown
453	lt shell grey
453 / 3782	lt shell grey / lt mocha brown
500	vy dk blue green
500 / 520	vy dk blue green / dk olive drab
501	dk blue green
501 / 3362	dk blue green / dk loden green
502 / 522	blue green / olive drab
502 / 3363	blue green / loden green
503 / 523	med blue green / med olive drab
504 / 524	lt blue green / lt olive drab
520	dk olive drab
522	olive drab
523	med olive drab
524	lt olive drab
640	vy dk beige grey
762	vy lt pearl grey
778 / 3747	lt antique mauve / vy lt blue violet

Cross Stitch

DMC	COLOR
930 / 3746	dk antique blue / dk blue violet
931	med antique blue
932	lt antique blue
3032 / 3045	med mocha brown / dk yellow beige
3033	vy lt mocha brown
3041	med antique violet
3041 / 3726	med antique violet / dk antique mauve
3042	lt antique violet
3045	dk yellow beige
3046	med yellow beige
3362	dk loden green
3363	loden green
3743	vy lt antique violet
3747	vy lt blue violet
3752	vy lt antique blue
3787	dk brown grey

DMC Rayon Floss

30543	ul vy lt beige brown
30712	cream

Backstitch

520	leaves
930	alphabets, numbers
3032	border rings, arch (**2** strands), heart border (**1** strand)

Note: Wrap 3032 in arch using 30543 (**1** strand).
Wrap 3032 in heart border using 30712 (**2** strands).

3787	columns, line under lettering (**2** strands)

Note: Wrap 3787 line under lettering using 30712 (**1** strand).

315	ribbons
640	all other

Lazy Daisy

501 / 3363	leaf clusters

Specialty Stitch

DMC	
3042	Algerian Eye Stitch
422 / 3033	Diamond Smyrna Stitch
422 / 3033	Eight-Sided Eyelet Stitch
422 / 3033	partial Eyelet Stitch
ecru	Satin Stitch (**3** strands)
778 / 3747	Satin Stitch (**2** strands) (**1** strand)
30712	Satin Stitch
30543	Satin Stitch
422 / 3033	Plaited Stitch (Heart Border, follow arrows)
3033	Rhodes Stitch (small squares at top of columns)

Mill Hill Glass Seed Beads

03005	platinum rose
03021	royal pearl

Attach platinum rose beads using 1 strand DMC 3042.
Attach royal pearl beads using 1 strand DMC ecru.
Add beads after all other stitching is complete.

WEDDING SAMPLER SECTION 1

Shaded row indicates overlap from Section 1.

WEDDING SAMPLER SECTION 2

Shaded rows indicate overlaps from Sections 2 and 3.

WEDDING SAMPLER SECTION 4

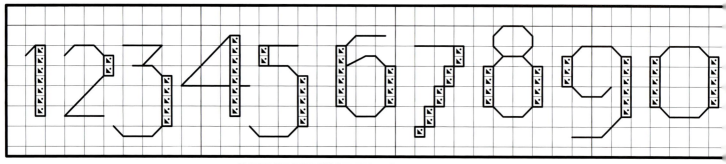

NUMBERS/OVER-ONE DETAIL

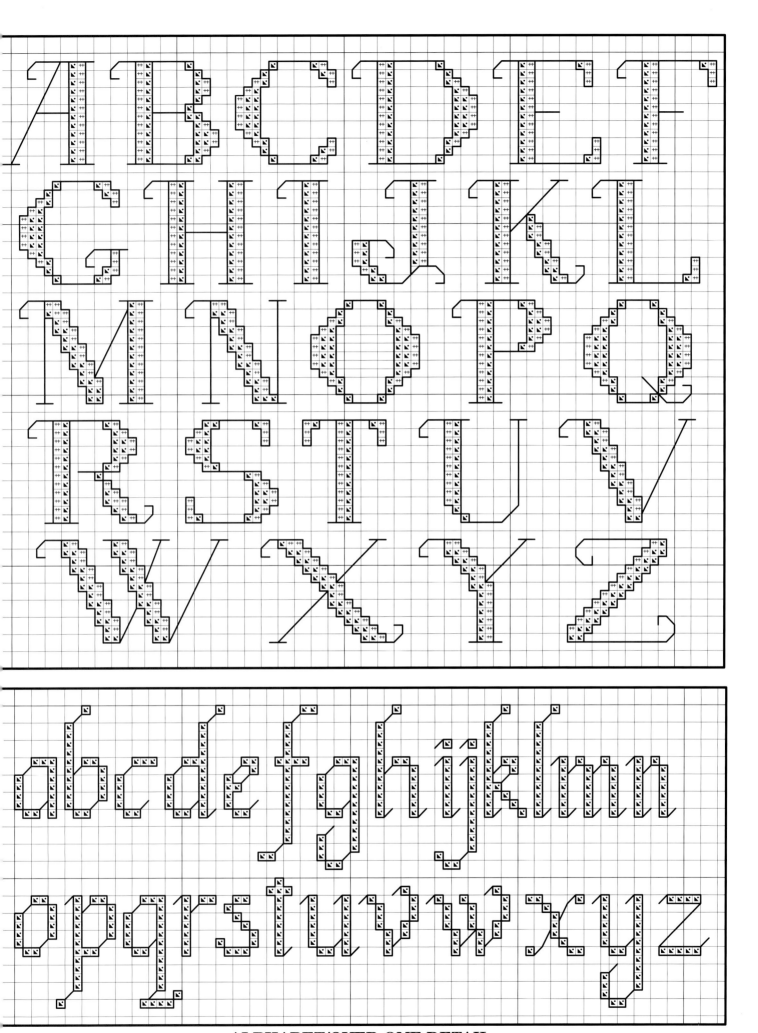

ALPHABET/OVER-ONE DETAIL

Heart Sampler

Our model was stitched over two fabric threads on 25 count Antique White Lugana fabric from Zweigart®, using 2 strands of floss for Cross Stitches and Specialty Stitches and 1 strand for Backstitches unless noted. Alphabet and numbers are provided for personalization. *We recommend stitching the design in the order listed. We stitched our model with silk fibers.*

Stitch Count: 90w x 120h
Design Size:
25 ct fabric (over 2 threads) $7\frac{1}{8}$" x $9\frac{1}{2}$"
28 ct fabric (over 2 threads) $6\frac{1}{2}$" x $8\frac{5}{8}$"
32 ct fabric (over 2 threads) $5\frac{5}{8}$" x $7\frac{1}{2}$"

Cross Stitch

KREINIK SOIE D'ALGER	DMC	COLOR
blanc	blanc	white
X 122	504	blue green
1011	225	pink
○ 1732	762	pearl grey
△ 2541	746	off white

DMC Pearl Cotton
blanc #8
blanc #12

MILL HILL GLASS SEED BEADS
• 00479   white
Attach using 1 strand of blanc floss.
Add beads after all other stitching is complete.

Outer Border
1. Cross Stitch border
2. blanc #8 pearl cotton — Satin Stitch
3. blanc #12 pearl cotton — Eyelet Stitch
4. 1011

Corner Motifs
1. blanc #8 pearl cotton — Satin Stitch
2. Cross Stitch corners
3. 1011 — Spider's Web in center of square

Knotted Cluster Border
1. blanc #12 pearl cotton — Hemstitch long edges
2. Using small, pointed scissors, carefully cut the ten threads that run crosswise in these areas, cutting close to the Satin Stitch bars. Remove cut threads without pulling fabric out of shape.
3. Using blanc #12 pearl cotton, anchor pearl cotton behind work at center of one of the Satin Stitch bars. Gather and knot three pairs of threads together, working across the row. Anchor pearl cotton at the end of the row.

Area A
1. □ blanc #12 pearl cotton — Four-Sided Stitch (do not pull threads)
2. Work Cross Stitch
3. blanc #8 pearl cotton — Satin Stitch
4. 1732
5. blanc — Queen Stitch

Area B
1. blanc #12 pearl cotton — Long-Armed Cross Stitch

Area C
1. Work Cross Stitch
2. 122 (**2** strands)
3. 1011 — Eyelet Stitch
4. blanc — Medium Diamond Eyelet Stitch
5. blanc #8 pearl cotton — Satin Stitch
6. 1732

Area D
blanc #12 pearl cotton — Herringbone Stitch

Area E
1. blanc — Small Diamond Eyelet Stitch
2. 1732
3. blanc #8 pearl cotton (long stitches)

Area F
1. blanc — Eyelet Stitch Variation
2. Work Cross Stitch
3. blanc #8 pearl cotton — Kloster Block
4. blanc #12 pearl cotton — Eyelet Stitch
5. Using small, pointed scissors, carefully cut threads following the pink dotted lines, cutting close to the Kloster Block bars. Remove cut threads without pulling fabric out of shape.
6. blanc #12 pearl cotton — Woven Bars
7. blanc #12 pearl cotton — Dove's Eye

Area G
1. 122 — Smyrna Cross Stitch
2. blanc #8 pearl cotton — Rice Stitch where boxes appear (legs 1-2 and 3-4 only)
3. blanc (**1** strand) — Rice Stitch (remaining legs)

Area H

blanc #12 pearl cotton — Montenegrin Cross Stitch

Area I

1. Work Cross Stitch
2. blanc #8 pearl cotton — Alternating Scotch Stitch
3. 1011 — Satin Stitch
4. 1732 — Satin Stitch

Area J

1. blanc #8 pearl cotton — Satin Stitch
2. Using small, pointed scissors, carefully cut the six threads that run crosswise in these areas, cutting close to the Satin Stitch bars. Remove cut threads without pulling fabric out of shape.
3. blanc #12 pearl cotton — Hemstitch (top)
4. blanc #12 pearl cotton — Serpentine Hemstitch (bottom)

Note: Catch four threads per cluster in the top row of hemstitching. In the bottom row, catch two threads in the first cluster, four threads across the row, and then two threads in the last cluster. This gives the trellis effect.

Area K

blanc — Horizontal Knitting Stitch

Area L (initial and date blocks)

1. blanc #8 pearl cotton — Satin Stitch
2. blanc #12 pearl cotton — Smyrna Cross Stitch
3. 122 (**2** strands) letters and numbers

Area M (large heart)

1. Work Cross Stitch
2. blanc #12 pearl cotton (long stitches)

Note: Being careful not to pull fabric out of shape; work stitches from top left to bottom right first; then work stitches from top right to bottom left, weaving over and under first stitches.

3. 122 — Upright Cross Stitch
4. 122
5. 1011

ALPHABET AND NUMBERS

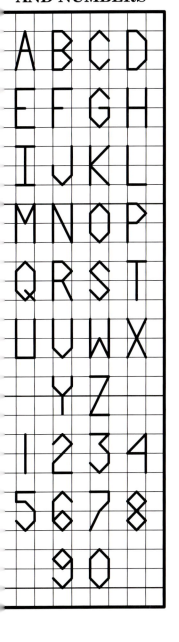

PLACEMENT DIAGRAM

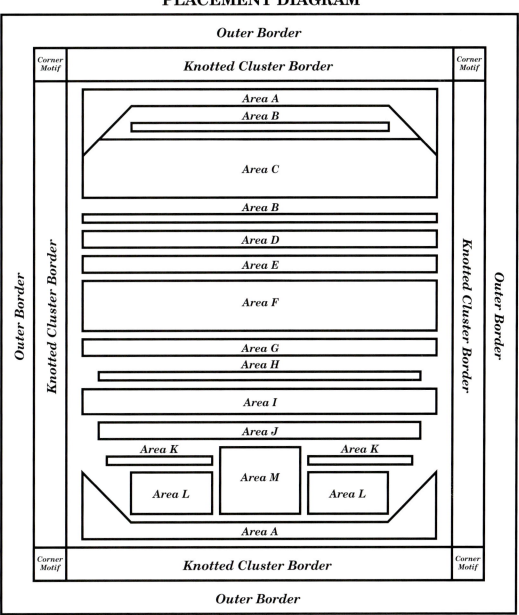

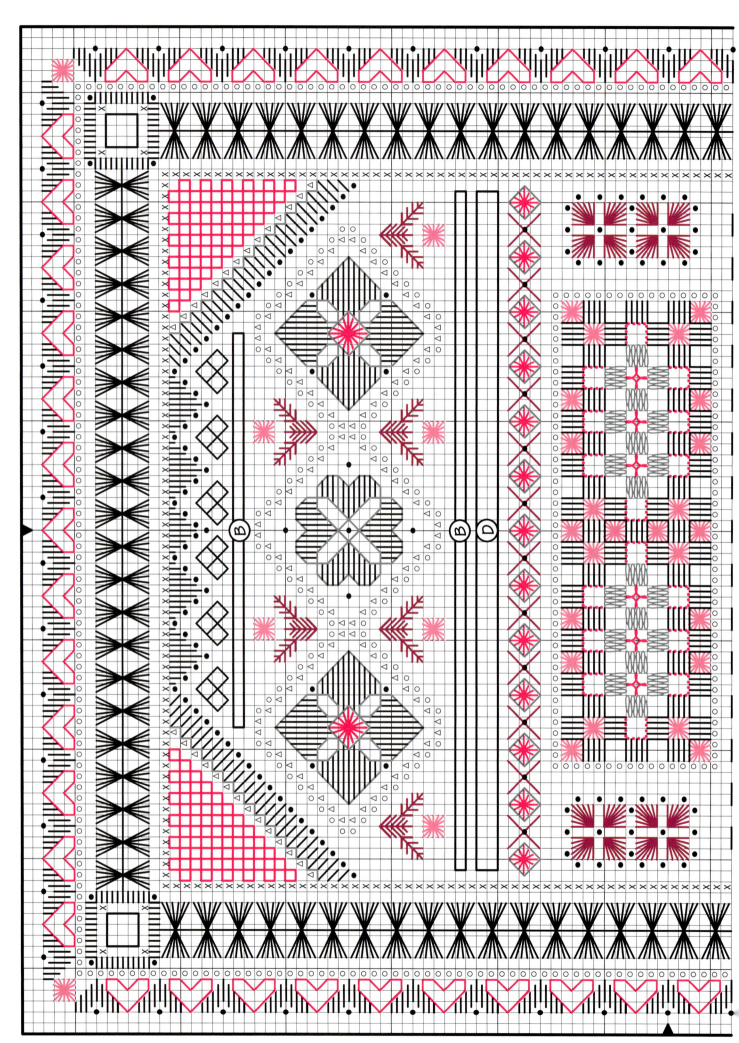

HEART SAMPLER SECTION 1

Shaded rows indicate overlap from Section 1.

HEART SAMPLER SECTION 2

GENERAL INSTRUCTIONS

CHART INFORMATION

The color key shows the symbols used for Cross Stitch in the chart. Blended Stitches are indicated by bracketing ([ ) two or more colors together. Each symbol on the chart represents one stitch. Backstitch, French Knot, Lazy Daisy Stitch, Specialty Stitch, and Bead instructions are also listed.

When a Backstitch, Lazy Daisy Stitch, or a bead is worked over a Cross Stitch, the symbol may be slightly smaller (or reduced and placed on both sides of the Backstitch or Lazy Daisy symbol).

When Quarter Stitches are to be used, different reduced symbols are shown on each side of the Backstitch.

Working over Two Fabric Threads

When working over two fabric threads, the stitches should be placed so that vertical fabric threads support each stitch. Make sure that the first Cross Stitch is placed on the fabric with stitch 1-2 beginning and ending where a vertical fabric thread crosses over a horizontal fabric thread.

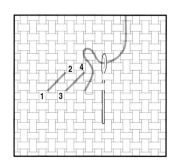

Beginning and Ending Stitches: Never tie knots in floss. Instead, cover floss tail on back of work with the first few stitches. To end stitching, run floss under complete stitches on back of fabric and clip remaining strands close to surface.

STITCH DIAGRAMS

CROSS STITCH
(over 2 fabric threads)

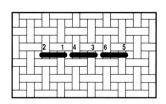

BACKSTITCH
(over 2 fabric threads)

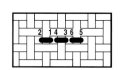

BACKSTITCH
(over 1 fabric thread)

HALF CROSS STITCH
(over 2 fabric threads)

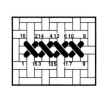

CROSS STITCH
(over 1 fabric thread)

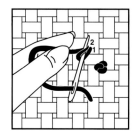

FRENCH KNOT

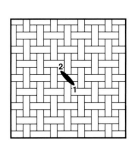

QUARTER STITCH
(over 2 fabric threads)

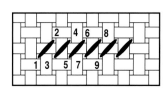

HALF CROSS STITCH
(over 1 fabric thread)

When working over one fabric thread on linen, do not pull floss too tight. This may cause stitches to be drawn behind fabric threads.

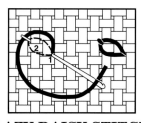

LAZY DAISY STITCH

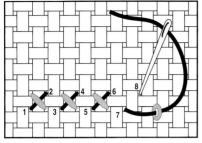
ATTACHING BEADS

MEDIUM DIAMOND EYELET STITCH

EIGHT-SIDED EYELET STITCH

ALGERIAN EYE STITCH

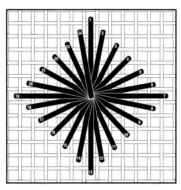
LARGE DIAMOND EYELET STITCH

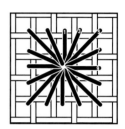
SMALL EYELET STITCH

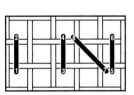
BARRIER STITCH

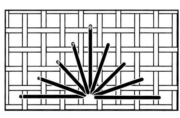
DIAMOND EYELET VARIATION STITCH (Partial Eyelet Stitch)

MEDIUM EYELET STITCH

CHAIN STITCH

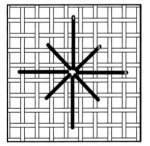
VERY SMALL DIAMOND EYELET STITCH

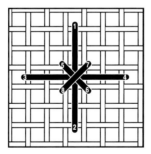
DIAMOND SMYRNA STITCH

LARGE EYELET STITCH

SMALL DIAMOND EYELET STITCH

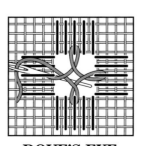
DOVE'S EYE

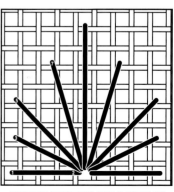
EYELET VARIATION STITCH 1

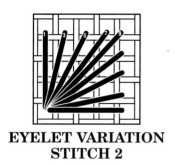

EYELET VARIATION STITCH 2

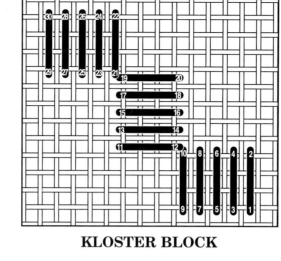

KLOSTER BLOCK

QUEEN STITCH

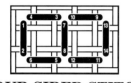

FOUR-SIDED STITCH

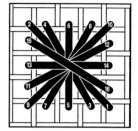

RHODES STITCH

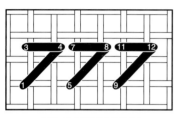

HEMSTITCH
(Christmas Sampler and English Garden Sampler)

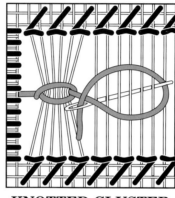

KNOTTED CLUSTER

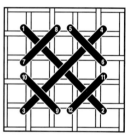

RICE STITCH

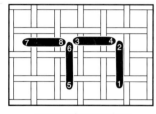

HEMSTITCH
(Heart Sampler – knotted cluster border)

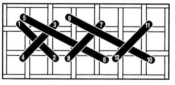

LONG-ARMED CROSS STITCH

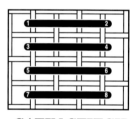

SATIN STITCH

HERRINGBONE STITCH

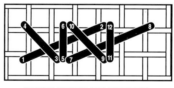

MONTENEGRIN CROSS STITCH

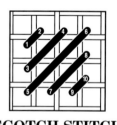

SCOTCH STITCH

HORIZONTAL KNITTING STITCH

PLAITED CROSS STITCH

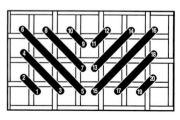

ALTERNATING SCOTCH STITCH